Praise for *The Starfish and the Spider*

"*The Starfish and the Spider* provides a powerful prism for understanding the patterns and potential of self-organizing systems."
—Steve Jurvetson, partner, Draper Fisher Jurvetson

"Ori and Rod provide sharp insights into how to avoid becoming the next victim of market populism; or if you are so inclined, the strategies to take on those vulnerable incumbents."
—Randy Komisar, author, Stanford professor, and
Kleiner Perkins Caufield and Byers partner

"It is amazing and continues to give me much to consider—something happens every other day that makes me think about the concepts. Bravo!"
—Jessica Flannery, cofounder, Kiva.org

"*The Starfish and the Spider* is great reading. [It has] not only stimulated my thinking, but as a result of the reading, I proposed ten action points for my own organization."
—Professor Klaus Schwab, executive chairman,
World Economic Forum

Ori Brafman is a lifelong entrepreneur. His adventures include a wireless start-up, a health-food advocacy group, and a network of CEOs working on public benefit projects, which he co-founded with Rod Beckstrom. He holds a BA in peace and conflict studies from the University of California at Berkeley and an MBA from Stanford Business School. He lives in San Francisco. Ori's Web site is www.oribrafman.com. He can be contacted for speaking via the Leson Agency at 609-235-5037 or larryleson @comcast.net.

Rod A. Beckstrom is chairman and chief catalyst of Twiki.Net, Inc. and founded CATS Software Inc., which he took public as CEO. Rod serves on the boards of Environmental Defense and Jamii Bora Africa Ltd. He holds a BA and an MBA from Stanford and was a Fulbright Scholar. He lives in Palo Alto, California and can be contacted through www.beckstrom.com. To arrange a speaking engagement for Rod, please contact the Penguin Speakers Bureau at speakersbureau@us.penguingroup.com.

The Starfish

and the Spider

The Unstoppable Power of
Leaderless Organizations

Ori Brafman and Rod A. Beckstrom

PORTFOLIO

PORTFOLIO

Published by the Penguin Group

Penguin Group (USA) Inc., 375 Hudson Street, New York, New York 10014, U.S.A.
Penguin Group (Canada), 90 Eglinton Avenue East, Suite 700,
Toronto, Ontario, Canada M4P 2Y3 (a division of Pearson Penguin Canada Inc.)
Penguin Books Ltd, 80 Strand, London WC2R 0RL, England
Penguin Ireland, 25 St Stephen's Green, Dublin 2, Ireland (a division of Penguin Books Ltd)
Penguin Group (Australia), 250 Camberwell Road,
Camberwell, Victoria 3124, Australia (a division of Pearson Australia Group Pty Ltd)
Penguin Books India Pvt Ltd, 11 Community Centre,
Panchsheel Park, New Delhi – 110 017, India
Penguin Group (NZ), 67 Apollo Drive, Rosedale,
North Shore 0632, New Zealand (a division of Pearson New Zealand Ltd)
Penguin Books (South Africa) (Pty) Ltd, 24 Sturdee Avenue,
Rosebank, Johannesburg 2196, South Africa

Penguin Books Ltd, Registered Offices: 80 Strand, London WC2R 0RL, England

First published in the United States of America by Portfolio, a member of
Penguin Group (USA) Inc. 2006
This paperback edition published 2007

20 19 18 17 16 15 14 13

Illustrations by Manuel Lima

Publisher's Note
This publication is designed to provide accurate and authoritative information in regard to the
subject matter covered. It is sold with the understanding that the publisher is not engaged in
rendering legal, accounting, or other professional services. If you require legal advice or
other expert assistance, you should seek the services of a competent professional.

THE LIBRARY OF CONGRESS HAS CATALOGED THE HARDCOVER EDITION AS FOLLOWS:
Brafman, Ori.
The starfish and the spider : the unstoppable power of leaderless organizations / Ori Brafman
and Rod A. Beckstrom.
p.   cm.
Includes index.
ISBN 1-59184-143-7 (hc.)
ISBN 978-1-59184-183-8 (pbk.)
1. Decentralization in management. 2. Organizational behavior. 3. Success in business.
I. Beckstrom, Rod A. II. Title.
HD50.B73   2006
302.3'5—dc22   2006046262

Printed in the United States of America
Set in Bembo with Akzidenz Grotesk • Designed by Sabrina Bowers

To Arif, who insisted that we write,
and to our families and friends for their support

CONTENTS

INTRODUCTION

It was like a game of Where's Waldo. But instead of kids playing the game, the players were the world's leading neuroscientists. And instead of Waldo, they were looking for a curly-haired, sweater-wearing grandma. Anyone's grandma.

The neuroscientists were trying to answer what at first appeared to be a simple question. We all have memories—whether of our first day at school or of our grandmother. But where, the scientists asked, do these memories reside? Little did they know that they were about to arrive at a conclusion that would have surprising implications, not only for biology but also for every industry in the world, for international terrorism, and for a host of far-flung communities.

Scientists had long assumed that our brains, like other complex machines, had a top-down structure. Surely, in order to store and manage a lifetime of memories, our brains needed a chain of command. The hippocampus is in charge, and neurons, which store specific memories, report up to it. When we recall a memory, our hippocampus, acting like a high-speed computer, retrieves it from a specific neuron. Want to access a memory of your first love? Go to neuron number 18,416. Want to access a memory of your fourth-grade teacher? Go to neuron number 46,124,394.

In order to prove this theory, the scientists needed to show that certain neurons are activated when we attempt to retrieve a particular memory. Beginning in the 1960s, scientists wired up subjects with electrodes and sensors and showed them pictures of familiar objects. The hope was that each time a subject was presented with a picture, a specific neuron would be triggered. Subjects spent hours staring at photos. The scientists watched and waited for specific neurons to fire. And they waited. And they waited.

Instead of a neat correlation between particular memories and particular neurons, they found a mess. Each time subjects were presented with a picture, many different neurons lit up. What's more, sometimes the same group of neurons would light up in response to more than one picture.

At first, the scientists figured that it was a technological problem—maybe the sensors weren't precise enough. For decades afterward, neuroscientists conducted variations on this experiment. Their equipment became more sensitive, but still they produced no meaningful results. What was going on? Surely, memories had to reside *somewhere* in the brain.

An MIT scientist by the name of Jerry Lettvin proposed a solution: the notion that a given memory lives within one cell was just plain wrong. As much as scientists wanted to find hierarchy in the brain, Lettvin argued, it just wasn't there. Lettvin's theory was that rather than being housed in particular neurons that report to the hippocampus, memory is distributed across various parts of the brain. He coined the term "grandmother cell" to represent the mythical neuron that houses the memory of grandma. The picture Lettvin painted of the brain at first appears primitive and disorganized. Why would such a complex thinking machine evolve in such an odd way?

Counterintuitive as it may be, this distributed structure actually makes the brain more resilient. Let's say, for example, we wanted to erase a certain memory from someone's brain. Under the hierarchical model, we'd locate the specific neuron and zap it, and the memory would be gone. But in Lettvin's model, the memory would be much more difficult to eliminate. We'd have to zap a *pattern* of neurons—a much more difficult proposition.

Like neuroscientists searching for the grandma cell, when we look at the world outside of our brain, we naturally seek order. We look for hierarchy all around us. Whether we're looking at a Fortune 500 company, an army, or a community, our natural reaction is to ask, "Who's in charge?"

This book is about what happens when there's no one in charge. It's about what happens when there's no hierarchy. You'd think there would be disorder, even chaos. But in many arenas, a lack of traditional leadership is giving rise to powerful groups that are turning industry and society upside down.

In short, there's a revolution raging all around us.

No one suspected that Shawn Fanning, sitting in his dorm

room at Northeastern University in 1999, was about to change the world. The eighteen-year-old freshman typed at his computer and wondered what would happen if people could share music files with one another. Fanning came up with Napster, an idea that would deliver a crushing blow to the recording industry. But he wasn't at the head of this attack—the entire battle was waged by an army of music-sharing teens, college students, and, eventually, iPod-carrying businessmen.

Half a world away, when Osama bin Laden left Saudi Arabia and traveled to Afghanistan, hardly anyone realized that in just a few years he would become the most wanted man in the world. At the time, his power appeared limited. After all, what could a man operating out of a cave really do? But al Qaeda became powerful *because* bin Laden never took a traditional leadership role.

In 1995 a shy engineer posted online listings of upcoming events in the San Francisco Bay Area. Craig Newmark never dreamed that the site he launched would forever alter the newspaper industry. In 2001 a retired options trader set out to provide free reference materials to kids around the world. He never thought that his efforts would one day allow millions of strangers to use something called a "wiki" to create the biggest information depository of our time.

The blows to the recording industry, the attacks of 9/11, and the success of online classifieds and a collaborative encyclopedia were all driven by the same hidden force. The harder you fight this force, the stronger it gets. The more chaotic it seems, the more resilient it is. The more you try to control it, the more unpredictable it becomes.

Decentralization has been lying dormant for thousands of

years. But the advent of the Internet has unleashed this force, knocking down traditional businesses, altering entire industries, affecting how we relate to each other, and influencing world politics. The absence of structure, leadership, and formal organization, once considered a weakness, has become a major asset. Seemingly chaotic groups have challenged and defeated established institutions. The rules of the game have changed.

This would become strikingly clear on the steps of the U.S. Supreme Court, where a high-profile case was about to become surprisingly weird.

CHAPTER 1

MGM's Mistake and

the Apache Mystery

Don Verrilli might as well have uncorked the champagne bottle right then and there on the marble steps of the Supreme Court—the case he was about to argue was a slam-dunk. It was late March 2005, and Verrilli must have felt like he was on top of the world.

Verrilli is the kind of lawyer you want on your side. He was the editor-in-chief of the prestigious *Columbia Law Review*, he clerked for Justice William Brennan, and he regularly wins big cases in front of the Supreme Court. The man is one serious overachiever. If Verrilli is like Babe Ruth, he was joined by an all-star legal team that resembled the 1927 New York Yankees: it included heavy-hitters Ken Starr (of Clinton impeachment and

Monica Lewinsky fame) and David Kendall (who defended Clinton during said impeachment). You wouldn't want to be playing against this lineup.

Verrilli and crew were the hired guns of MGM, the huge entertainment company. MGM, in turn, was joined in the suit by giants like Columbia, Disney, Warner Brothers, Atlantic Records, Capitol Records, RCA, BMG, Sony, and Virgin Records.

You get the idea: the biggest players, with the best lawyers in the world, arguing before the highest court in the land. And what were these giants fighting? Grokster, a tiny company that most of us have never even heard of.

Grokster is what's referred to as a P2P (peer-to-peer) service. It allows people to steal—ahem, share—music and movie files over the Internet. Given how easy the service was to use, and given that it was completely free, people from all over the world had been happily sharing everything from the latest Britney Spears album to the hottest unofficial movie releases. In fact, *Star Wars Episode III: Revenge of the Sith* appeared online on P2P networks for free the same day it was released in movie theaters.

The only catch was that none of this content was licensed. Grokster's users were basically stealing music. And we're not just talking about a few hackers sitting in the dark basements of university computer science departments. We're talking about Average Joe living down the block. In fact, if you ask any eighteen- to twenty-four-year-old with access to a computer, chances are they've used a service like Grokster. It's estimated that there were 8.63 million users of P2P services in the United States alone in April 2005.

There hadn't been so much sharing by young people in

America since the Summer of Love days in 1968. All this swap-ping was adding up to trouble for the film and recording indus-tries. MGM and its fellow labels weren't in the business of letting music and film proliferate around the world; they were trying to make a profit. Music-swapping was having a significant im-pact on the bottom line. Just how much? Verrilli would tell us soon.

The counselor began his oral argument but was interrupted by Justice Breyer, who saw an elephant going to pieces over a tiny mouse. He asked, essentially, what's the big deal? "There is innovation," he said to Verrilli, "and there are problems in the music industry, but it thrives, and so forth."

Verrilli saved his response for the very end of his oral argu-ment. He knew that the elephant he was representing wasn't just being hysterical. It had good reason to be scared out of its wits. "Justice Breyer," Verrilli pleaded, "the facts are that we have lost—the recording industry has lost—25 percent of its revenue since the onslaught of these services."

Twenty-five percent. That's something to get worked up about.

The entire mess had started only five years before the Supreme Court case, when a no-name college freshman was too lazy to go to Tower Records. Lazy or arrogant, he wanted his music for free. Eighteen-year-old Shawn Fanning, nicknamed "Napster" by his friends, launched a company out of his dorm room. Peo-ple used Napster by logging into a central server and sharing files with others around the world. Everyone loved the invention and started swapping files like there was no tomorrow.

And sure enough, there wasn't much of a tomorrow for

Napster. The labels quickly slapped Napster with a lawsuit. Un-surprisingly, groups like the ACLU protested that the suit was a free speech violation, but the courts didn't buy that argument. Nor did anyone pay much attention to the countless angry hackers who, like children who'd just lost a schoolyard brawl, taunted, "We'll get you—it's just gonna get worse for you!"

Indeed, on February 12, 2000, the courts ruled against Napster. In June 2003, Napster declared bankruptcy, and in December 2003 it sold its brand name and intellectual property to Roxio, Inc., for a song.

All this legal wrangling was part of a larger strategy. Let's say the locksmith down the street is running an entire business centered on ripping you off. In the morning, as soon as you leave for work, the locksmith sneaks up the stairs to your house, breaks the lock, and props the door open. Everyone and his uncle barges in, checks out your silverware, your dishes, your jewelry, your new stereo, and walks out with them. A couple of burly guys even carry off your washing machine.

You come home, and after the initial shock wears off, you want to go after both the burglars and the people who let them in. The record labels were faced with a similar problem. The P2P companies were enabling theft, and users were pirating music left and right.

The industry came up with a two-pronged strategy. First they went after the specific thieves—in this case, the people who were swapping the music. They tracked down those people who were downloading songs—the big offenders—and slapped them with a copyright infringement lawsuit, threatening to take them to court unless they settled and paid a $4,000 fine. This tactic was meant not only to deter file-swappers from ever downloading a song again but also to send a strong message to the rest of the world: we're serious about enforcing our intellectual property rights. If you break the law and steal our content, we'll go after you.

Second, the labels attacked the root of the problem by going after the people who were picking the locks and enabling the theft—in this case, the P2P companies. The labels retained the best lawyers to sue these companies out of existence. Enter Verrilli. As expected, the attorney performed flawlessly. It's not a big surprise that two months after his oral argument, the court handed down a unanimous decision in MGM's favor.

But as the labels were repeatedly winning lawsuits against P2P companies, the overall problem of music piracy was getting worse and worse. It wasn't that the labels weren't vigilant enough. It was actually the opposite—the labels were adding fuel to the fire with every new lawsuit. The harder they fought, the stronger the opposition grew. Something weird was going on.

The best explanation for the events comes from an unlikely source. Meet Tom Nevins, a cultural anthropologist specializing in Native American tribes of the Southwest. Although Nevins has never set foot inside a recording studio, his study of ancient tribes sheds light on what's happening today in the music industry. In many ways, he understands what's going on better than anyone else.

We initially heard about Tom when we were leafing through the introduction he wrote to a book on the Apaches. Suddenly we stopped. Wait a second, we thought, this guy is talking about Native Americans, but what he's saying could just as easily apply to the Grokster case.

We tracked down Nevins in Iowa, where the young anthropologist was living with his wife and baby. At first, he was caught off guard. "Um," he said, "I didn't think anyone even read that book." But as we talked to him, Nevins started drawing connections, putting what was happening in the world in a much larger context.

It all starts with a mystery, an ancient mystery, and solving it provides the key to understanding where MGM went wrong. To uncover the solution, Nevins took us back in time almost five centuries, to the year 1519, to the land known today as Mexico City, where one of the most famous explorers in history, the legendary Hernando Cortés, set eyes on the Aztec capital for the very first time.

The explorer was amazed by the great highways leading to the metropolis—then called Tenochtitlán—as well as by the complex aqueducts and the sheer size and beauty of the temples and pyramids. Cortés had expected to see savages, but instead he encountered a civilization with a population of more than 15 million, its own language, an advanced calendar, and a central government. "The city," he marveled, "is as large as Seville or Cordoba," and in the marketplace "over 60,000 souls gather to buy and sell [and] one can behold every possible kind of merchandise found in lands the world over."

But Cortés didn't go to Tenochtitlán to sightsee. Like the CEOs of the record labels, Cortés was there to get rich. The way to get rich at that time was to get your hands on gold. And so one of the first things Cortés did was to speak with the Aztec leader, Montezuma II. He entered Montezuma's grand palace, which was big enough to house the entire Spanish army. The conversation he had can be summed up as follows: "Give me all your gold, or I'll kill you."

Montezuma didn't quite know what to do with the explorer. He'd never seen someone like him before, and on the off-chance that Cortés was a deity, Montezuma yielded and handed over all of his gold.

But just as no one has ever called Cortés a tourist, no one has ever called him a man of his word. Despite his promise, Cortés killed Montezuma. Chaos ensued. Cortés and his army surrounded Tenochtitlán. They barricaded the roads, preventing any food from entering the city, and they blocked off the aqueducts. Within eighty days, 240,000 inhabitants of the city starved to death.

By 1521, just two years after Cortés first laid eyes on Tenochtitlán, the entire Aztec empire—a civilization that traced its roots to centuries before the time of Christ—had collapsed. The Aztecs weren't alone. A similar fate befell the Incas. The Spanish army, led by Francisco Pizarro, captured the Inca leader Atahuallpa in 1532. A year later, with all the Inca gold in hand, the Spanish executed Atahuallpa and appointed a puppet ruler. Again, the annihilation of an entire society took only two years.

These monumental events eventually gave the Spanish control of the continent. By the 1680s, the Spanish forces seemed unstoppable. With the winds of victory at their backs, they headed north and encountered the Apaches. This meeting—in the deserts of present-day New Mexico—is crucially linked with the music industry's fight against the P2P sites. Why? Because the Spanish lost.

They lost to a people who at first seemed primitive. Unlike the Aztecs and the Incas, the Apaches hadn't put up a single pyramid, paved a single highway, or even built a town to speak of. More important for the conquistadors than pyramids or highways, the Apaches also had no gold. So, instead of pillaging, the Spanish tried to turn these people into Catholic farmers by forcing them to adopt an agrarian lifestyle and converting them to Christianity. Some of the Apaches did in fact take up rake and hoe, but the vast majority resisted. Not only did they resist, but they actively fought back—raiding everything in sight that was remotely Spanish.

You'd think that against an army like the Spanish, the Apaches wouldn't have had a chance. But that wasn't the case. As Nevins told us, "By the late seventeenth century, the Spanish had lost effective control of northern Sonora and Chihuahua to the Apaches. The Apaches had successfully wrested control of North Mexico—not that it was ever their desire to do so." This wasn't a single accidental victory, however. The Apaches continued to hold off the Spanish for another two centuries.

It wasn't that the Apaches had some secret weapon that was unknown to the Incas and the Aztecs. Nor had the Spanish army lost its might. No, the Apache defeat of the Spanish was all about the way the Apaches were organized as a society. The Spanish couldn't defeat them for the same reason that the record labels weren't able to squash the P2P trend.

Nevins told us how he arrived at the solution to the mystery. A few years ago, he spent three years living with the White Mountain Apaches in Arizona, studying their culture, observing their rituals, and learning how their society really works. He immediately recognized differences between the Apaches and other tribes: "If you look, for example, at the Sioux—the *Dances with Wolves* people, right?—they had some degree of political centralization. They resisted spectacularly for short periods of time, but they were really not successful for more than ten years. Whereas

the Apaches were fighting this battle for hundreds of years."
How did they survive? "They distributed political power and had
very little centralization." The Apaches persevered because they
were decentralized.

To understand the implications of what Nevins says, let's take
a quick look at two opposite systems. Centralized and decentralized. A centralized organization is easy to understand. Think of
any major company or governmental agency. You have a clear
leader who's in charge, and there's a specific place where decisions are made (the boardroom, the corporate headquarters, city
hall). Nevins calls this organizational type *coercive* because the leaders call the shots: when a CEO fires you, you're out. When Cortés
ordered his army to march, they marched. The Spanish, Aztecs,
and Incas were all centralized, or coercive. Although it sounds like
something out of a Russian gulag, a coercive system is not necessarily bad. Whether you're a Spanish general, an Aztec leader,
or a CEO of a Fortune 500 company, you use command-and-
control to keep order in your organization, to make it efficient,
and to function from day to day. Rules need to be set and enforced, or the system collapses. For instance, when you get on an
airplane, you had better hope it's a coercive system. You certainly
don't want Johnson from seat 28J to decide that right about now
is a good time to land. No, Johnson needs to sit quietly and
enjoy the movie while the captain—and only the captain—has
the authority to make decisions to ensure that the plane flies
properly.

Decentralized systems, on the other hand, are a little trickier
to understand. In a decentralized organization, there's no clear
leader, no hierarchy, and no headquarters. If and when a leader
does emerge, that person has little power over others. The best

that person can do to influence people is to lead by example. Nevins calls this an *open* system, because everyone is entitled to make his or her own decisions. This doesn't mean that a decentralized system is the same as anarchy. There are rules and norms, but these aren't enforced by any one person. Rather, the power is distributed among all the people and across geographic regions. Basically, there's no Tenochtitlán, and no Montezuma.

But without a Montezuma, how do you lead? Instead of a chief, the Apaches had a Nant'an—a spiritual and cultural leader. The Nant'an led by example and held no coercive power. Tribe members followed the Nant'an because they wanted to, not because they had to. One of the most famous Nant'ans in history was Geronimo, who defended his people against the American forces for decades. Geronimo never commanded an army. Rather, he himself started fighting, and everyone around him joined in. The idea was, "If Geronimo is taking arms, maybe it's a good idea. Geronimo's been right in the past, so it makes sense to fight alongside him." You wanted to follow Geronimo? You followed Geronimo. You didn't want to follow him? Then you didn't. The power lay with each individual—you were free to do what you wanted. The phrase "you should" doesn't even exist in the Apache language. Coercion is a foreign concept.

The Nant'ans were crucial to the well-being of this open system, but decentralization affects more than just leadership. Because there was no capital and no central command post, Apache decisions were made all over the place. A raid on a Spanish settlement, for example, could be conceived in one place, organized in another, and carried out in yet another. You never knew where the Apaches would be coming from. In one sense, there was no place where important decisions were made, and in another sense, decisions were made by everybody everywhere.

On first impression, it may sound like the Apaches were loosey-goosey and disorganized. In reality, however, they were an advanced and sophisticated society—it's just that a decentralized organization is a completely different creature. Nevins explained that the traits of a decentralized society—flexibility, shared power, ambiguity—made the Apaches immune to attacks that would have destroyed a centralized society.

Let's see what happens when a coercive system takes on an open system. The Spanish (a centralized body) had been used to seeing everything through the lens of a centralized, or coercive, system. When they encountered the Apaches, they went with the tactics that had worked in the past (the take-the-gold-and-kill-the-leader strategy) and started eliminating Nant'ans. But as soon as they killed one off, a new Nant'an would emerge. The strategy failed because no one person was essential to the overall well-being of Apache society.

Not only did the Apaches survive the Spanish attacks, but amazingly, the attacks served to make them even stronger. When the Spanish attacked them, the Apaches became even more decentralized and even more difficult to conquer. When the Spanish destroyed their villages, the Apaches might have surrendered if the villages had been crucial to their society. But they weren't. Instead, the Apaches abandoned their old houses and became nomads. (Try to catch us now.)

This is the first major principle of decentralization: *when attacked, a decentralized organization tends to become even more open and decentralized.*

Back in our twenty-first-century reenactment of the conflict, the music labels took on the role of the Spanish. The part of the Aztecs was played by P2P companies like Grokster and Napster. The labels slapped on lawsuits and brought in modern-day conquistadors like Verrilli. As we saw, these tactics worked, and Napster went out of business. The labels defeated Napster because it was more centralized than not. The company had a Tenochtitlán (central servers that users had to log into) and a Montezuma (a hierarchical structure with a CEO). In other words, although Napster was more open and decentralized than the labels (it allowed users to swap music for free with other users), it wasn't decentralized and flexible enough to withstand attacks by the centralized giants. By crippling the Tenochtitlán (Napster's central server) and going after Montezuma (Napster's corporate management), the music labels prevailed.

But Napster's destruction didn't quell people's desire for free music. Imagine that you're a kid who's been drinking from the fountain of free downloaded music. All of a sudden, some guys in suits turn off the spigot and declare you a criminal. Sure, you can go back to the record store—a place you haven't seen for months—and shell out three hours' salary for a CD. A more attractive option, however, is to find a Napster equivalent.

Along came Niklas Zennstrom, a Swedish engineer, who wanted to make it big by feeding the hungry—the hungry song-swappers, that is. Zennstrom was no Apache Nant'an, but he realized that in order to survive he had better avoid Napster's mistakes. His solution was a new program called Kazaa. With Kazaa, there's no central server, no Tenochtitlán. John in California could directly access Denise's computer in Nebraska for that brand-new U2 song or Jerry's computer in San Francisco for that favorite Beatles tune. Within twelve months, more than 250 million copies of Kazaa had been downloaded. The avalanche of music-swapping was massive. Kazaa gave power to the users without the need for a central server.

Compare Kazaa to the record labels. The record labels have offices, distribution channels, marketing departments, and high-paid executives. Because they have exclusive content, they can charge users a premium. And no, you can't copy a CD and give it to your friends. Kazaa, on the other hand, is like an Apache village. There are no headquarters, no big salaries, and if you want to make a thousand copies of your favorite song, by all means go right ahead.

But in order to have a business you need a Montezuma, right? Zennstrom, wanting to stay off the labels' radar, was at best a reluctant Montezuma: he built pyramids only when he thought the labels weren't looking, and he paved roads only in places where the labels didn't have much access. His revenue came from selling ad space on Kazaa, a centralized feature that proved to be a weakness. Zennstrom was so wary of companies like MGM, in fact, that he and his partner eluded men on motorcycles, representatives of the record labels, who tried to serve them with subpoenas.

When the labels, acting like the Spanish, finally succeeded in suing Kazaa and its users, Zennstrom sold the Dutch parent company to an outfit based on the South Pacific island of Vanuatu—far beyond the reach of the American and European legal systems. Just like the Apaches, who had no choice but to become nomadic, Zennstrom had to be decentralized to survive.

He was never able to cash out. Nant'ans were never in the habit of getting rich. But don't cry for Zennstrom; as we'll see later, getting sued out of the music business was the best thing that ever happened to him.

A similar cat-and-mouse game ensued between the labels and companies like Grokster and eDonkey, which closely resembled Kazaa. Remember Verrilli? By the time he argued MGM's case against Grokster in 2005, the record labels' strategy had two huge problems. Not only was it ineffective, but it was making the problem worse.

As Chris Gorog, the current CEO of Napster II (which bought the name from Napster), explains: "Pirating will always be out there, but it will probably be considered pretty edgy and wrong. Parents are being very vigilant." So that means that the lawsuits *are* making a difference, right? Not exactly. Chris concedes that "there are statistics that show that pirating is down a little bit, but I don't think it's materially down." The record labels may convince themselves that the strategy works, but in reality it's far from solving the problem.

Not only is the music industry unable to curb pirating, but, in accord with the first principle of decentralization, every time the labels sue a Napster or a Kazaa, a new player comes onto the scene that's even more decentralized and more difficult to battle. For example, after Kazaa was chased out to the South Pacific, an unknown hacker made the service even more open and decentralized. The hacker took the Kazaa software, erased the parts that served ads and generated revenues, and distributed this new version online. This new, more decentralized version of Kazaa is known as Kazaa Lite or K+. Millions began downloading Kazaa Lite. The same thing happened with eDonkey, a company that offered a service like Kazaa's. Meet eDonkey's illegitimate child, eMule, a knockoff that is eating into the other players' market share and managing to get on every company's nerves. Why? Because eMule is more decentralized than anything anyone in the music business has seen—the software is a completely open-source solution. No owner. No Montezuma. Who started eMule? No one knows. They simply can't be found. Sam Yagan, head of eDonkey, explains that "eMule is a rogue network, it's open-source, there's no way for them to pursue the entity eMule." And he's speaking from experience: "If anybody has had incentive to go find the eMule guys and shut them down, it's been us, you know, over the last three years, but we—we can't find them. And we're insiders in the industry, you know."

The diagram below shows how the P2P players are becoming more and more open and decentralized—and more difficult to control and battle.

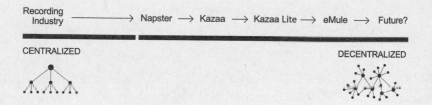

Companies like eMule are so decentralized that they are beyond the reach of any label's lawyer. Who would you sue—the software? There is not even a trace of a leader. You'd think eMule doesn't even exist, except that it's hacking away at everyone's profits.

So what's an MGM CEO to do? Sam Yagan and the guys at eDonkey offered to start charging their users for the service and sharing revenues with the labels—basically, to go legit with a subscription model. But the labels wouldn't hear of it. Instead, they are busy looking for ways to survive. As the Napster II CEO puts it, "The record labels have been out there for about a hundred years. And for a hundred years they've been paying the artists cents on the dollar, if that. They are starting to try to recharacterize what they do for a living as marketing companies, but you know, how many times have you seen print ads or TV ads or outdoor billboards for music artists? Rarely. They're going to be completely disintermediated at some point."

It seems like everyone associated with the labels is losing money. Well, almost everyone. As Sam tells us, "You have to remember who's making money right now in this whole process over the last few years—hands down, it's the lawyers." Don Verrilli isn't complaining. For lawyers, it's a lot of the same old same old—more and more lawsuits.

For the record industry, however, things will never be the same. Yes, they can hire Verrilli, who is the best of the best. And yes, they have a mountain of resources that they can throw at the problem. But frankly, it doesn't much matter. Companies like Grokster are enabling the theft of intellectual property. But it doesn't help that the Supreme Court rules unanimously in MGM's favor.

The harder you fight a decentralized opponent, the stronger it gets. The labels had the power to annihilate Napster and destroy Kazaa. But waging that battle was possibly the *worst* strategic move the labels made. It started a chain reaction that now threatens the entire industry. As the labels go after the Napsters and Kazaas of the world, little programs like eMule start popping up.

Now, it's not that MGM and the other labels are stupid, nor are they alone. It's just that MGM hasn't stopped to fully understand this new force. What we've seen with the P2P companies is just the tip of the iceberg.

CHAPTER 2

The Spider, the Starfish, and the

President of the Internet

It was 1995, and Dave Garrison had a problem. He'd just been hired as the CEO of Netcom, an early Internet service provider (ISP) like AOL or Earthlink. The problem: Dave knew nothing about the Internet. He had another problem too: he had to raise money from bankers who knew even less about the new technology than he did.

Sitting by the beach in Santa Cruz, California, ten years later, Dave tells us the story. "I was actually recruited into the Internet space by a headhunting firm in Palo Alto [in Silicon Valley]. I didn't understand what the Internet was, but at the time, the company was running out of cash, and we had to go back to the public market for a secondary round of fund-raising. So I was learning about it in the limousine between fund-raisings."

Remember, in 1995 the few people who even knew what the term "online" meant were having enough trouble navigating Web pages ("How do I go 'back'?"), let alone figuring out the architecture of the entire Net. By the time Dave arrived in Paris, his limo tutorials had him sounding like a pro. "The best part was in France at a Michelin restaurant in one of the top hotels in Paris. There were about thirty people in the room, all very well dressed, speaking in hushed tones—the antithesis of dot-com shorts and T-shirts. It felt to me like I was seen as an American curiosity piece from California. It was like they were hearing fantastic tales from this young American about some computer that will change the world. But then we got stumped. One of the investors started asking who was the president of the Internet. We went in circles about how 'there is no president.' So it was very . . . it was very funny. But this is 1995, early '95, so the Internet is still an unknown thing. We're explaining, 'It's a network of networks,' and, 'Imagine what it would be like if all the customers of a department store could organize in a fashion and share information, and it shifts the balance of power.' We're laying this stuff out, and people are like, 'Who are these guys? What drugs are you on?' It was very interesting because we didn't know what it could mean. But we just knew it was fundamental—a way of connecting communities that was very different."

Dave's explanations were far from satisfactory to the French investors. If they were going to shell out cash for a public offering, they wanted to make sure that someone was in charge, to ensure that this wasn't a chaotic system. They needed a Cortés. They probably would have settled for a Montezuma. But Dave didn't deliver. Instead, he and the investors continued going around and around. The concept was just too foreign to the French. They started getting angry.

Dave recalls that their questions were "based on the concept of 'It has to be centralized, there has to be a king, or there has to be an emperor, or there has to be a—something.' These key investors—"probably thirty people in a room in one of the five-star hotels," Dave recalls—were a "very intelligent group of people," but they didn't get it. Dave tried another approach: the Internet was a network of networks. "We said, 'There are thirty to forty thousand networks, and they all share in the burden of communication.' And they said, 'But who decides?' And we said, 'No one decides. It's a standard that people subscribe to. No one decides.' And they kept coming back, saying, 'You don't under-stand the question, it must be lost in translation, who is the president of the Internet?' And honestly, I, I—I tried to be very up front in describing [it] the best way [I could], but I was deeply unable to."

Eventually Dave surrendered. He gave the French what they wanted. "I said *I* was the president of the Internet, 'cause other-wise we weren't going to get through with the sales spiel. I wasn't trying to be flippant. I wanted to move on, I wanted to sell secu-rities. So I will tell you, I was the first president of the Internet, claimed so in Paris. Absolutely, I was."

Now, Dave's French investors weren't flat-earthers. The Inter-net, after all, was a brand-new technology at the time. They had a right to be concerned, and it was good that they asked so many questions. But the interaction does point to a common human trait: when we're used to seeing something in a certain way, it's hard to imagine it being any other way. If we're used to seeing the world through a centralized lens, decentralized organizations don't make much sense. It was difficult for the French investors to comprehend the new Internet technology because no part of it fit the way they viewed the world. The French, like the Spanish two hundred years before them, were used to seeing things in a particular way: organizations have structures, rules, hierarchies, and, of course, a president.

Just as history provides an explanation of MGM's predicament, nature explains the French investor quandary. In a nutshell, the French mistook a starfish for a spider.

Most of us know that a spider is a creature with eight legs coming out of a central body. With a magnifying glass, we can see that a spider also has a tiny head and eight eyes. If the French investors were to ask who was running the spider show, the answer is clearly the head. If you chop off the spider's head, it dies. It could maybe survive without a leg or two, and could possibly even stand to lose a couple of eyes, but it certainly couldn't survive without its head. It's no surprise, then, that when the French investors first heard of the Internet, they wanted to know who was in charge—where was the head? It's one of the most important questions to ask about a centralized organization.

But when learning about the Internet, the French investors weren't dealing with a spider. They were actually encountering a starfish. At first glance, a starfish is similar to a spider in appearance. Like the spider, the starfish appears to have a bunch of legs coming out of a central body. But that's where the similarities end. See, the starfish is Tom Nevins's kind of animal—it's decentralized.

With a spider, what you see is pretty much what you get. A body's a body, a head's a head, and a leg's a leg. But starfish are very different. The starfish doesn't have a head. Its central body isn't even in charge. In fact, the major organs are replicated throughout each and every arm. If you cut the starfish in half, you'll be in for a surprise: the animal won't die, and pretty soon you'll have two starfish to deal with.

Starfish have an incredible quality to them: If you cut an arm off, most of these animals grow a new arm. And with some varieties, such as the Linckia, or long-armed starfish, the animal can replicate itself from just a single piece of an arm. You can cut the Linckia into a bunch of pieces, and each one will regenerate into a whole new starfish. They can achieve this magical regeneration because in reality, a starfish is a neural network—basically a network of cells. Instead of having a head, like a spider, the starfish functions as a decentralized network. Get this: for the starfish to move, one of the arms must convince the other arms that it's a good idea to do so. The arm starts moving, and then—in a process that no one fully understands—the other arms cooperate and move as well. The brain doesn't "yea" or "nay" the decision. In truth, there isn't even a brain to declare a "yea" or "nay." The starfish doesn't have a brain. There is no central command. Biologists are still scratching their heads over how this creature operates, but it makes perfect sense in Tom Nevins's worldview. The starfish operates a lot like the Nant'ans. If spiders are the Aztecs of the animal world, starfish are surely the Apaches.

Living in a world of spiders, it was hard for the French investors to fully understand the starfish, let alone appreciate its potential. That's why they needed a president of the Internet.

And this brings us to the second principle of decentralization: *it's easy to mistake starfish for spiders.* When we first encounter a collection of file-swapping teenagers, or a native tribe in the Arizona desert, their power is easy to overlook. We need an entirely different set of tools in order to understand them.

Let's look at one of the best-known starfish of them all. In 1935 Bill Wilson was clenching a can of beer; he'd been holding a beer, or an alcoholic variation thereof, for the better part of two decades. Finally, his doctor told him that unless he stopped drinking, he shouldn't expect to live more than six months. That rattled Bill, but not enough to stop him. An addiction is hard to overcome.

Bill was trapped. You'd think he'd have turned to the experts, but they had been of no help. Well meaning as they were, none had a cure for alcoholism. They'd come up with a host of remedies, but all were ineffective. So there was Bill, feeling ashamed, scared of dying, and, above all, hopeless. Something needed to change.

It was then that Bill had a huge insight. He already knew that he couldn't combat alcoholism all by himself. And experts were useless to him because he and other addicts like him were just too smart for their own good. As soon as someone told him what to do, Bill would rationalize away the advice and pick up a drink instead. It was on this point that the breakthrough came. Bill realized that he could get help from other people who were in the same predicament. Other people with the same problem would be equals. It's easy to rebel against a shrink. It's much harder to dismiss your peers.

Alcoholics Anonymous was born.

At Alcoholics Anonymous, no one's in charge. And yet, at the same time, everyone's in charge. It's Nevins's open system in action. The organization functions just like a starfish. You automatically become part of the leadership—an arm of the starfish, if you will—the moment you join. Thus, AA is constantly changing form as new members come in and others leave. The one thing that does remain constant is the recovery principle—the famous twelve steps. Because there is no one in charge, everyone is responsible for keeping themselves—and everyone else—on track. Even seniority doesn't matter that much: you're always an alcoholic. You have a sponsor, like a Nant'an, but the sponsor doesn't lead by coercion; that person leads by example. And if you mess up and relapse or stop attending for a while, you're always welcome to come back. There's no application form, and nobody owns AA.

Nobody owns AA. Bill realized this when the group became a huge success and people from all over the world wanted to start their own chapters. Bill had a crucial decision to make. He could go with the spider option and control what the chapters could and couldn't do. Under this scenario, he'd have had to manage the brand and train applicants in the AA methodology. Or he could go with the starfish approach and get out of the way. Bill chose the latter. He let go.

He trusted each chapter to do what it thought was right. And so, today, whether you're in Anchorage, Alaska, or Santiago, Chile, you can find an AA meeting. And if you feel like it, you can start your own. Members have always been able to directly help each other without asking permission or getting approval from Bill W. or anyone else. This quality enables open systems to quickly adapt and respond.

Compare that with what happened in the Florida Keys during

one of the worst storms in recorded history, known today as the Labor Day hurricane of 1935. As the storm came closer and closer, meteorologists optimistically predicted that it wouldn't hit the Keys. But retired major Ed Sheeran had a different view. Sheeran was a supervisor for an FDR public works project with more than four hundred workers. Sheeran had lived through a hurricane earlier in the century, and everything in his gut told him there was something to worry about. But he didn't just rely on his gut: his barometer confirmed his fears. He saw clear signs that the storm was heading right for the Keys.

Sheeran raised a flag and told his supervisor, who called headquarters in Jacksonville and told them that he was concerned and didn't want to take a chance. The best move, he argued, was to evacuate the workers. Headquarters was sympathetic and arranged a rescue train to go down to the Keys. The only problem was that no one bothered to inform the workers that they should get on it.

Realizing that the train had come and gone, Sheeran fired another warning: we need to evacuate these workers now! His alerts eventually worked their way up the chain of command, but headquarters—once bitten—decided that instead of deploying another train, the best thing would be to sit and wait. Sheeran might be overreacting, and if conditions did indeed worsen, a train could always be dispatched from Miami. Meanwhile, the U.S. Weather Bureau contended that Sheeran was making much ado about nothing.

Unfortunately, Sheeran was right. The hurricane hit with massive force and 160-mile-per-hour winds. By the time headquarters finally approved a rescue effort, it was too late. The window of opportunity was gone. When a second rescue train was dispatched, the hurricane blew it off the tracks. Two hundred fifty-nine workers died in the storm.

There were obvious advantages to FDR's centralized government. It was able to save millions from starvation and reverse a crippling depression. But FDR's government, like our own today, was too centralized to respond quickly to the stranded workers. As in 2005 when Hurricane Katrina flooded New Orleans, those on the ground had the best knowledge, but they were powerless to implement large-scale rescue plans. Instead, before the spider could react, information had to be relayed up to the head, and then the head had to process the information, strategize, and finally react. Viewed from this perspective, what happened in 1935 in the Keys and in 2005 in New Orleans wasn't necessarily any one individual's fault. Yes, some individuals could have made better decisions, but the real culprit each time was the system itself. It's times like these that you need a starfish.

If Sheeran had been operating in an open system, he would have been able to lead by example and take action. When both his gut and his barometer forecast bad news, he could have told people, "I'm getting out of here. Anybody who wants to join me is welcome." He would then have been able to organize a hurricane escape effort without having to convince higher-ups in Jacksonville that his experience and barometer readings were valid. Now, Sheeran could have also been wrong, in which case the workers would have been evacuated unnecessarily. It's not that open systems necessarily make better decisions. It's just that they're able to respond more quickly because each member has access to knowledge and the ability to make direct use of it.

This brings us to the third principle of decentralization: *an open system doesn't have central intelligence; the intelligence is spread throughout the system.* Information and knowledge naturally filter in at the edges, closer to where the action is.

Let's go back to AA and Bill W.'s decision to adopt a starfish approach. Turns out Bill made the right strategic decision. The open system was the way to go. It has helped countless people. Literally. Today, if you were to ask how many members AA has, there'd be no way to tell. How many chapters? Again, no way to tell. No one knows, because AA is an open system. There's no central command keeping tabs. AA is flexible, equal, and constantly mutating. When other addicts took note of AA's success, they borrowed the twelve-step model and launched organizations combating a variety of addictions, including narcotics, food, and gambling. AA's response? Good for you. Go right ahead. It's all a part of the design. The fourth principle of decentralization is that *open systems can easily mutate.*

AA has transcended Bill W.'s original vision and grown into a surprisingly strong and lasting organization, a lot like the Apaches, in fact. The Apaches did not—and could not—plan ahead about how to deal with the European invaders, but once the Spanish showed up, Apache society easily mutated. They went from living in villages to being nomads. The decision didn't have to be approved by headquarters. It was easy to execute because Apache society was open. Likewise, it never occurred to Bill W. that his treatment for alcoholism would help gamblers and food addicts. Again, Bill W. didn't execute any control mechanism. As soon as an outside force presents itself, the decentralized organization quickly mutates to meet the new challenge or need.

AA has a lot in common with eMule. Bill W., like the anonymous hacker who launched eMule, was no CEO. Rather, Bill served to catalyze a new idea and then got out of the way. He left his organization without a central brain and, in so doing, gave it the power to mutate and continually alter its form.

Let's see how this plays out on the corporate battlefield. Napster comes on the scene and deals a blow to the record labels. From then on, the open and coercive systems engage in a conflict of radically different responses. At the labels, each decision needs to be analyzed and approved by the executives. Meanwhile, the P2P networks are reacting at blazing speed, constantly mutating and staying a step ahead of the labels. Containing this series of mutations is like capturing mercury. You put down Napster, Kazaa pops up. You get rid of Kazaa, Kazaa Lite emerges, and so forth. Although the small P2P companies don't have many resources at their disposal, they're able to react and mutate at a frighteningly quick pace. This spells trouble for a spider organization that sees starfish circling around it.

Whether you're a spider or just an observer on the battlefield, eventually you'll realize the fifth principle of decentralization: *the decentralized organization sneaks up on you.* Because the decentralized organization mutates so quickly, it can also grow incredibly quickly. Spider organizations weave their webs over long periods of time, slowly amassing resources and becoming more centralized. But the starfish can take over an entire industry in the blink of an eye. For hundreds of years, people turned to experts to combat alcoholism, and then, within just a few years, AA was founded and became the accepted way of digging out of addiction. Since the Industrial Revolution, people had communicated by mail, telegraph, or telephone, but the Internet changed everything in less than a decade.

For a century, the recording industry was owned by a handful of corporations, and then a bunch of hackers altered the face of the industry. We'll see this pattern repeat itself across different sectors and in different industries. We call this radical swing "the accordion principle." Over time, industries swing from being decentralized to centralized to decentralized and back again. In response to overcentralized industries or institutions, people rebel and create open starfish systems. In fact, some of these systems, like eMule, are so decentralized that in many ways they no longer look like an organization: eMule is highly distributed, and members have a high degree of freedom. At the extreme of decentralization, we encounter a gray zone where a very loose collection of people have a surprising amount of power.

To see how this plays out, let's go back to the nineteenth century, when the power of the music industry was held by live performing musicians, musicians like the violinist Joseph Joachim. During the 1830s, while the Mexicans were busy fighting the Apaches in America, little Joseph Joachim was practicing his violin in Europe. Joachim's teachers could spot true talent, and the student excelled. Eventually the young violinist landed an impressive mentor, the famous composer Felix Mendelssohn.

To break into the nineteenth-century music scene, a musician had to be an impressive performer. Joachim was exactly that. When he traveled to London with Mendelssohn, he received an exceptionally warm response. Londoners couldn't get enough of him, but when Joachim left town, he took his virtuosity with him. Decades before the advent of recorded music, you couldn't purchase his greatest hits.

In 1887 Thomas Edison figured out how to play back sound and invented the phonograph. This changed everything: now you could take music home with you. With people listening to more and more records, hundreds of little recording studios started up. The power of the industry began to shift. Instead of independent musicians holding the power, a recording studio could discover a new talent and market a given record on the radio and in stores.

This marked the birth of the record deal. To make it as a serious musician, you now had to get a label to recognize your talent and invest in you. A few big industry players emerged, and the music industry became more centralized.

Compare Joachim's career with that of Itzhak Perlman. Perlman was born in 1945, about forty years after Joachim died, and the same year that the phonograph industry first surpassed sheet music in total revenues. Like Joachim, Perlman was recognized as a unique talent. Just as Joachim had debuted in London, Perlman stunned audiences in Carnegie Hall. That's where the similarities end. Unlike Joachim, Perlman has a fan base the majority of whom have never seen him perform live. Perlman's career, like that of other big-time modern musicians, was made possible by the big labels. By the end of the twentieth century, 80 percent of the global record industry was concentrated among five labels: Sony, EMI, BMG, Universal Music, and Warner Brothers. There weren't many small labels left, and those that somehow managed to flourish were quickly scooped up and acquired by the Big Five. Over the course of a hundred years, music labels gained massive power, and small labels and independent musicians were squeezed out.

Then, as we've seen, Shawn Fanning's Napster shook up the industry. It took only five years for a century-old industry to get turned on its head. The power radically shifted—from the spider-like big labels to starfishlike companies such as Grokster and eMule. That's an example of the decentralized revolution in action.

Take a look at the progression of the music industry over 115 years below. Notice that in 1890 the market was dominated by artists. In the next snapshot, 1945, the independent record labels came onto the scene. They both increased the overall revenue of the industry and reduced the artists' market share—the money in 1945 was in record deals. No one got rich from Joachim's playing in the 1800s, but as the industry became more and more centralized, companies could capture more revenues: whereas before the phonograph Joachim could play to an audience of a

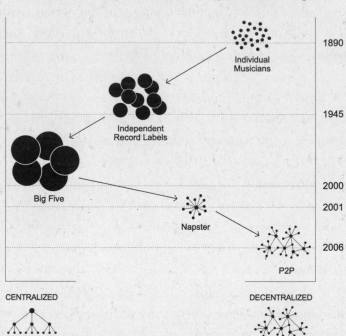

The Music Industry: From Starfish to Spider and Back Again

thousand, now Perlman records could be sold to millions—with a healthy profit for the label on each sale. By the end of the twentieth century, the shift was even more pronounced. The 2000 snapshot depicts an industry that had undergone gradual but massive centralization. The Big Five had the vast majority of market share and were making good profits. We know what happened in 2001—that's when Napster entered the scene. By 2005, the industry was vastly different. Sony and BMG had consolidated, Tower Records had filed for bankruptcy, and teenagers were no longer flocking to CD shops to get the latest music. The combined revenues of the remaining four giants were 25 percent less than they had been in 2001. Where did this revenue go?

Not to the P2P players. The revenues disappeared. Starfish organizations may not have been raking in the dough (with one big exception we'll see in the next chapter), but they were decreasing overall industry revenues. This is the sixth principle of decentralization: *as industries become decentralized, overall profits decrease.* Introduce starfish into the equation and wave good-bye to high profits. It's why you want to be on the lookout for any starfish before they take an industry by storm.

The trick is, of course, to predict explosive change before it occurs. As the French investors could tell you, differentiating a starfish from a spider isn't easy when you're not prepared for it. Especially when you're not asking the right questions. That's precisely what MGM and the record labels have been doing: falling into the French investor pitfall over and over again. When French investors—or, for that matter, Spanish generals or heads of big record labels—encounter an open system, they lift up the lid and look inside. When they don't see a central nervous system, they either dismiss the organism or treat it as an inconsequential spider.

So how do we avoid the French investor pitfall? By asking the right questions.

1. Is there a person in charge?

A coercive system depends on order and hierarchy. There's always a pyramid, and there's always someone in charge. In short, if you see a CEO, chances are you're looking at a spider. An open system, on the other hand, is flat. There's no pyramid for anyone to sit on top of.

Obviously, MGM has a CEO. He calls the shots and decides which markets to enter, what strategic path to pursue, and which P2P company to go after next. There's hierarchy and there's clear accountability—even the CEO must report to the board.

The Apaches, on the other hand, didn't make any centralized decisions, let alone have someone in charge. Nant'ans could make suggestions, but they didn't give orders to anyone. Likewise, Bill W. founded AA, but he got out of the way pretty quickly. Not only does eMule lack a CEO, no one even knows who originated it. And as the French investors eventually realized—sorry, Dave—the Internet doesn't have a president.

2. Are there headquarters?

Every spider organization has a physical headquarters. A headquarters is so integral that if we don't know whether a company is for real or not, we often check whether it has a physical address. No one orders priceless jewels, after all, from some company that has only a PO box.

You want to go visit the CEO of MGM? Pack your bags and head to Los Angeles. You want to visit the head of eMule? Good luck. A starfish organization doesn't depend on a permanent location or a central headquarters. Yes, AA has a physical address and lists its offices in New York. But that's not really where AA exists. The organization is equally distributed across thousands of community centers, churches, even airports. AA is found wherever a group of members chooses to meet.

3. If you thump it on the head, will it die?

If you chop off a spider's head, it dies. If you take out the corporate headquarters, chances are you'll kill a spider organization. That's why assassins go after the president of a country and armies invade capitals. Average Joe in Missouri is probably safe from an attempt on his life.

Starfish often don't have a head to chop off. When the Spanish started killing Nant'ans, new ones took their places. When Bill W. died, AA continued to thrive. If the record labels finally get their hands on the creator of eMule, the program will continue as though nothing ever happened.

4. Is there a clear division of roles?

Most centralized organizations are divided into departments, and the divisions between departments are rather firm. Marketing does marketing, human resources does human resources, and so on. Each department's role and responsibilities are pretty much fixed. Some departments take on multidisciplinary roles, but, at the end of the day, each has its own distinct function. A department is a leg of the spider. In a healthy spider organization, each leg is steady and helps to support the weight of the organization.

In decentralized organizations, anyone can do anything. A part of a decentralized organization is akin to a starfish arm: it doesn't have to report to any head of the company and is responsible only for itself. If a member of AA wants to start a new circle, or if a member of eMule wants to post thousands of new songs, they can. Any and every activity is within anyone's job description.

5. If you take out a unit, is the organization harmed?

Units of a decentralized organization are by definition completely autonomous. Cut off a unit and, like a starfish, the organization generally does just fine. In fact, the severed arm might grow an entirely new organization. Isolate an AA circle from the AA organization, and both will be able to survive. The isolated circle may even create a new addict-support organization. What if you destroyed half the Web sites on the Internet? It would still survive. What if you took away 95 percent? Again, the system would persevere—in fact, it was designed to withstand a nuclear attack. Likewise, take a chunk out of a P2P network and you might have fewer songs for a while, but soon the network would rebuild itself.

In a centralized organization, every department is important. What happens if a spider loses a leg? The spider's mobility is significantly affected, and if it keeps losing legs, its survival will be at risk. Separate a company's accounting department from the rest of the organization and it won't magically sprout a whole new organization to support. Take out a manufacturing company's factory, and you cause irreparable damage.

6. Are knowledge and power concentrated or distributed?

In spider companies, power and knowledge are concentrated at the top. The person in charge is assumed to be the most knowledgeable and has the power to make key decisions. When the 1935 hurricane hit the Keys, it was assumed that the U.S. Weather Bureau had the best knowledge and was empowered to make the call about how to react to the coming storm.

In starfish organizations, power is spread throughout. Each member is assumed to be equally knowledgeable and has power equal to that of any other member. Each AA circle knows about the needs of its members, and each group can decide how to react accordingly.

7. Is the organization flexible or rigid?

Decentralized organizations are very amorphous and fluid. Because power and knowledge are distributed, individual units quickly respond to a multitude of internal and external forces—they are constantly spreading, growing, shrinking, mutating, dying off, and reemerging. This quality makes them very flexible. Think of the Internet: each day thousands of new Web sites emerge and countless others fade away. Likewise, AA quickly mutated into other organizations as soon as the need arose. It doesn't matter how big AA gets or how much history it has; any portion of the organization can easily mutate at the drop of a hat. Because the arms of the starfish have relative freedom, they can go in a multitude of directions.

Centralized organizations depend more on structure, and that tends to make them more rigid. A couple of bank employees, for example, can't decide one day to sell lemonade at their local branch instead of home loans.

8. Can you count the employees or participants?

It is possible to count the members of any spider organization; just check the payroll, membership rosters, or other records. Even secretive organizations, like the CIA, which usually keep employment information classified, know how many agents or members they have. With access to the right existing information, even an outsider can get a rough estimate of total employees.

Counting the members of starfish organizations, though, is usually an impossible task. It's not only that no one's keeping track, but also that anyone can become a member of an open organization—or likewise withdraw their membership—at any time. How many people are using the Internet right now? That's impossible to answer. At best you could hope to approximate how many computers are connected to the Internet. But how many people are actually using the Internet? And how many people are sitting at one particular computer station? More difficult yet is to figure out how many people use the Internet overall. The recent estimate of 950 million is really just a statistical guess. Even if theoretically you could survey everyone and get a precise number, that number would be inaccurate within a few milliseconds as someone brand-new to the Internet logged on.

Likewise, the Spanish army could tell you how many troops it had but never quite knew how many Apaches were out there. And who knows how many AA chapters are active worldwide, or how many people are using eMule at any given time?

9. Are working groups funded by the organization, or are they self-funding?

Because they are autonomous, the units of a decentralized organization are almost always self-funding. In open organizations, there is often no central well of money. Individual units might receive funding from outside sources, but they are largely responsible for acquiring and managing those funds.

Things are different on the centralized end of the spectrum. While some departments produce profits, others traditionally incur costs. Headquarters redistributes revenues, ensuring that each department is adequately funded. Without central funding, departments cannot survive. If MGM, for example, decided to cut its entire marketing budget, the department would quickly die.

10. Do working groups communicate directly or through intermediaries?

Typically, important information in centralized organizations is processed through headquarters. In the 1935 hurricane, for example, Sheeran had to communicate his concerns to the folks in Jacksonville, who then made the decision about whether or not to contact the train operators. Likewise, in a typical firm the marketing department might conduct a study on the sales of a given product, then communicate the information to the company's executives, who would then decide how to respond to the market demands and instruct the factory to increase or decrease production.

The Soviet government took this concept to an extreme. If a resident of Urengoy made a phone call to a friend in Tazovskiy, a hundred miles to the north, the call would be routed through Moscow, more than a thousand miles to the east. All phone calls were routed through Moscow. Why? The Kremlin wanted to keep tabs on what you were talking about—whether plotting to overthrow the government or locating spare parts for your tractor. The Soviets weren't the first, or the last, to keep central control of communication lines. Even the Roman empire, though spread around the world, maintained a highly centralized transportation system, giving rise to the expression "All roads lead to Rome."

In open systems, on the other hand, communication occurs directly between members. Whether you're an Apache or an eMule user, you can communicate with other members directly. No roads lead to Rome because there isn't a Rome; you couldn't route your phone calls through Moscow even if you wanted to.

The Spanish Army

	Centralization	Decentralization	
There's someone in charge	X		There's no one in charge
There are headquarters	X	.	There are no headquarters
If you thump it on the head, it dies	X		If you thump it on the head, it survives
There's a clear division of roles	X		There's an amorphous division of roles
If you take out a unit, the organization is harmed	X		If you take out a unit, the organization is unharmed
Knowledge and power are concentrated	X		Knowledge and power are distributed
The organization is rigid	X		The organization is flexible
Units are funded by the organization	X		Units are self-funding
You can count the participants	X		You cannot count the participants
Working groups communicate through intermediaries		X	Working groups communicate with each other directly

CENTRALIZATION	9	1	DECENTRALIZATION

The Apache

There's someone in charge	X	There's no one in charge
There are headquarters	X	There are no headquarters
If you thump it on the head, it dies	X	If you thump it on the head, it survives
There's a clear division of roles	X	There's an amorphous division of roles
If you take out a unit, the organization is harmed	X	If you take out a unit, the organization is unharmed
Knowledge and power are concentrated	X	Knowledge and power are distributed
The organization is rigid	X	The organization is flexible
Units are funded by the organization	X	Units are self-funding
You can count the participants	X	You cannot count the participants
Working groups communicate through intermediaries	X	Working groups communicate with each other directly

CENTRALIZATION	1	9	DECENTRALIZATION

CHAPTER 3

A Sea of Starfish

What do an encyclopedia, a piece of software, a phone company, classified ads, and naked people in the Nevada desert have in common?

You guessed it: they're all decentralized.

There's a sea of starfish out there—now that we can appreciate their power and complexity, let's take a dive.

Skype

If you recall, the last time we visited Niklas Zennstrom, he was dodging men on black motorcycles with subpoenas in their hands.

The Kazaa founder was experiencing some serious legal problems, and finally he would have enough. Zennstrom passed the baton to some South Sea Islanders who set up shop on Vanuatu. It was now their turn to run. Indeed, when we tried to chase down Nikki Hemming, the current CEO of Kazaa, in Sydney, the closest we got was her next-door neighbor. Despite the neighbor's pleading, she wasn't willing to meet with us. The music industry lawyers had her under siege.

Yes, the record labels only made things worse for themselves, and soon more decentralized players came onto the scene. But as for Zennstrom, he was out of a job and needed to find a new project.

As proven by the advent of eMule, there really wasn't much money—if any—in creating P2P file-sharing programs. There's a catch-22, in fact. To make money from file-swapping programs, you need to make them somewhat centralized so that you can serve up ads or charge users a fee. To collect money, you generally need to have an account somewhere, which leads to centralization. But the moment you have any central office, the moment you start drawing a profit, companies like MGM come after you. Hence the dilemma: either be somewhat centralized and face lawsuits, or be completely decentralized but produce no revenues.

Zennstrom started looking for other industries where he could apply P2P technologies. He found his calling in the telephone industry. Just as people prefer to have free music, they also love to have free phone conversations. For years, hackers had concocted schemes to talk on the phone for free. But each of these schemes was illegal—they were using the phone company's lines, after all, and it had a right to be paid.

The phone companies, like the record labels, hadn't changed much in the hundred years before the advent of the Internet. Making a long-distance phone call used to involve connecting to an operator, who'd connect you to other operators, who'd eventually connect you to your relative in El Paso, Texas. With automation, the operators were replaced by computers and the phone lines were sometimes replaced by satellites or fiber-optic cables. But it was still the same centralized system.

Because the phone companies controlled the lines, you had to pay them whatever they wanted, or whatever regulators would allow them to charge. It used to be that AT&T was the only player in the United States. Then in 1984 the courts broke the company up and created some competition among various long-distance providers. You now had more choice, but you still had to choose between almost identical services. You had to use the phone company's lines—there was no way around it.

Until the Internet and Zennstrom came onto the scene, that is. Here was Zennstrom's idea: take the lesson from Kazaa—avoid central servers. Zennstrom's new company, Skype, let people connect to each other directly. No servers routing calls, no telephone lines to worry about. As a bonus, this time Zennstrom was going to do it within the confines of the law.

Meanwhile, Skype's users were getting a great deal. They got to communicate freely with any other Skype user in the world without ever having to rely on a phone line. All a user had to do was download some free software from Skype and plug a headset into his PC. Everything was done over the Internet. It didn't cost a cent. A user paid only a few pennies (.017 euros, to be exact) when the call terminated in an old-fashioned land line.

Unsurprisingly, a lot of people loved the service and quickly gravitated to it. When we met with Zennstrom in December 2004, Skype had 15 million users. By the end of 2005, it had 57 million.

But Skype's innovation didn't stop there. Zennstrom figured out a way to drive the cost of adding a new member down to zero. That's because Zennstrom decentralized the user database.

In the old days, to get a phone number you'd call 411 and have the operator check the directory. But Skype didn't maintain a central user listing. The listing itself was broken up into tiny pieces—each of which resided on users' computers. Each user, that is, hosted a tiny portion of the overall directory on his own machine—so you might be the host, for example, of listings "Webb" through "Wernstein." In true open fashion, everyone contributed to the network. The pieces were replicated multiple times across computers around the world. The brilliance of this open system was that Skype avoided the costs of storing names on its own servers. The only transactions that ever hit Skype servers were credit card payments.

In pushing the cost of calls to zero, Skype rendered the telephone industry's models of generating profits through long-distance charges obsolete. As Michael Powell, then chairman of the Federal Communications Commission (FCC), told *Forbes* in 2004: "I knew it was over when I downloaded Skype, when the inventors of Kazaa are distributing for free a little program that you can use to talk to anybody else, and the quality is fantastic, and it's free—it's over. The world will change now inevitably."

David Dorman, former CEO of AT&T, explained to us how the traditional phone companies were being affected by innovations like Skype. Skype didn't have to pay anything for calls made between members, and there was no tax on calls made over the Internet—Michael Powell, the FCC chairman, made sure of that. Skype paid nothing by the minute to connect, whereas traditional long-distance companies paid three cents a minute. Three cents a minute adds up quickly: AT&T and the other long-distance carriers were paying $20 billion per year.

Local phone companies weren't in a much better position. They had to maintain all of the costly infrastructure associated with handling a call—everything from phone cables to operator facilities. Skype bore none of these costs.

Skype capitalized on new technological advances to offer a previously monopolized privilege for free. This spells bad news for the traditional phone companies. It requires only a small amount of software to create a desktop system that works like Skype. The barrier to entry for becoming a long-distance provider, once huge and insurmountable, is quickly disappearing. Anyone with a few million dollars to invest can build a Skype-equivalent. Thus, although Skype may or may not thrive in the long run, it has opened a Pandora's box. How have the long-distance companies reacted? Taking a cue from the record labels, the big players began consolidating. Only a couple of months after we talked to David Dorman, SBC acquired AT&T.

As for Zennstrom, he's no longer running from men on motorcycles. More likely he's busy counting the billions that eBay paid to purchase Skype. We'll take a look at eBay's strategic decision to purchase Skype a little later. But first, let's look at another eBay investment.

Craigslist

By the time we walked up the steps of the old Victorian in San Francisco, we were expecting to see a saint. Everything we knew about Craig Newmark and his Web site craigslist, where people sell or trade virtually anything imaginable, was golden. We loved how craigslist was a perfect example of an open system. We'd heard that Craig cared most about the users and gave them the ultimate freedom, and that no one at craigslist was really in it for the money—but the site was pulling a profit nonetheless.

We first poked our heads into an office where eight or ten engineers were sitting around two rows of tables. There was a big sign reading PRIVATE. PLEASE DON'T WALK IN. We asked, "Is Craig here?" One of the engineers barely lifted his head and mumbled, "Upstairs."

We went up another level and walked to the very back of the dark house-turned-office. Craig's office was small by any account, and he shared it with Jim Buckmaster, the company's CEO. We walked in, and Craig greeted us with a smile. Jim was busy typing at his computer and didn't turn around. After a few minutes, he gave us a nod and turned back to his computer.

The interview started out all right. Craig told us that he was actually in charge of customer service. It really did seem like his biggest concern was supporting his users. Fame and fortune weren't at the forefront of his mind. In fact, the company was an accidental success. Craig told us that the site was founded in 1995, when he kept an e-mail list for local San Francisco Bay Area events. More and more people started posting to the list, and eventually it began taking up all of Craig's time. He seemed to have mixed feelings about being in charge of everything.

Despite Craig's ambivalence, the site has grown to massive proportions: craigslist is now found in 35 countries and more, than 175 cities around the world. The site attracts three billion page views a month. You can advertise and find virtually anything imaginable on craigslist—from garage sale items to used cars to houses to the love of your life—and it's all free. The only things that cost money are the job listings posted by for-profit companies. (Nonprofits get to post for free.) It's estimated that craigslist generates at least $10 million a year.

With so much traffic, we asked Craig, why don't you have any ads on the site?

Jim swiveled his chair back and quickly interjected: "Our users didn't ask for banner ads or text ads."

What do you mean? we asked.

Microsoft had approached them about banner ads, making "a lucrative offer," but craigslist turned them down, Jim explained. Why?

Craig responded: "The way craigslist runs is that people who use it post, and if they find something inappropriate they flag it for approval. So in a very day-to-day kind of way, the people who use the site run it. Also, in terms of policy, the categories we have almost one hundred percent were generated by people in the community. We tried to figure out what people were asking for, what was the consensus—what really worked—and we moved on that. I think that the initial idea over ten-plus years was mine. The rest of it was just listening to people and providing the infrastructure to that. Another thing is a culture of trust that works out really well."

Craig is right: there is a sense of trust on the site. The Web site allows users to interact with each other directly without anybody telling anybody else what they can and cannot do. No intermediaries, no bosses. But the big attraction to the site isn't just free ads. It's community. Virtually everyone we've talked to who has used craigslist refers to the site as a community, a place from another era when neighbors would help each other out. And craigslist does feel like a neighborhood. Like any neighborhood, it's home to all types—good and bad. People can post at will, but if something is offensive, for whatever reason, users themselves can take down the ad. It's a fully user-controlled democratic system.

This neighborhood is also an efficient marketplace. We ourselves have used craigslist for things like getting tickets to a Santana concert, selling a Web camera, buying a used computer for a friend, and finding a fiddle teacher. But the most memorable posting occurred when Ori moved and had a bunch of empty U-Haul boxes he wanted to get rid of. He posted an ad on craigslist's "free stuff" category, saying he had about a hundred boxes anyone could have for free. After immediately getting eight or nine responses, he e-mailed back to the first person who'd contacted him. An hour later a man named Glenn showed up at Ori's door, remarking on how helpful the boxes would be to him. "You know, when you move, costs just add up." Then he said something very small, but for some reason it struck a chord. "After I move, I'll be doing the same—passing the boxes on. You'll see them on craigslist soon."

It wasn't that Glenn was being hugely generous, nor that he had a big creative idea. It was just how Glenn talked about it. As if passing on the boxes were the most natural thing in the world. When you get free boxes from craigslist, you sort of owe one to the community, so of course you pass them along. That's what Craig was talking about—a sense of trust and community.

We understood that Craig valued the community. But still, we wanted to know, even just for the sake of argument, what was his business strategy? Would he eventually sell the company? Would he cash out? Would he ever start capitalizing on the traffic?

As we asked him these hypothetical questions, Craig looked down and then at his desk. It was as if we were offending him just by asking these questions. We had that awkward *What did we say?* feeling.

Craig said, "Jim, why don't you answer that question." As Jim gave us his response (essentially "We ain't selling to no one"), Craig focused on a stack of unopened mail. The second half of our recorded interview was largely obscured by the sound of Craig ripping open all his envelopes. When he was done, Craig logged on to his computer and began responding to e-mails.

When we left the Victorian thirty minutes later, we were a little taken aback—and surprised. What had happened? Then we realized that all along we'd been talking about how open systems are about the users, not about the leadership. In an open system, what matters most isn't the CEO but whether the leadership is trusting enough of members to leave them alone. For one reason or another—either because he trusts users or because he's reluctant to grow his company, or both—Craig does have reverence for his users. He lets them be.

We learned an important lesson—from the user perspective, people don't notice or care whether they're interacting with a spider or with a starfish. As long as they're given freedom, as long as they can do what they want to do, they're happy.

Over time, Craig's response has come to make a lot more sense to us. For one thing, he's a self-described introvert; conducting interviews with strangers isn't his idea of fun. But on a deeper level, Craig doesn't sell his users out. Getting out of their way and offering them what they're asking for has created the level of trust and community that everyone talks about. And after all, Craig is a customer service guy. He avoided our questions, tuned us out, and went back to what was really important—replying to e-mail from customers who in all likelihood weren't paying him a single penny.

One thing is for sure, though. Craigslist has had a devastating impact on newspaper revenues. In a move that is becoming familiar, the centralized players in the industry have reacted by consolidating—becoming more centralized. Merger talks between Village Voice Media (owner of several weeklies such as the *Village Voice* and *L.A. Weekly*) and New Times Corporation (the parent company of *East Bay Express*, *Phoenix New Times*, and *Denver Westword*) can be seen as a response to dwindling ad revenues. In its announcement, Village Voice Media touted its new effort to compete with craigslist with a site called backpage. com (referring to the alluring ads in the backs of most weekly publications). In a format that looks suspiciously like craigslist, backpage.com offers pretty much the same services as craigslist with the option of paying for the ad to be listed in print as well. This new site has a fraction of the number of viewers enjoyed by craigslist, and we're not holding our breath for backpage.com to become a major competitor to craigslist.

In a surprising twist, several weeks after we conducted the interview with Craig, we read that craigslist was now opposed to "scraping." Scraping is when one Web site lifts content from another. Many smaller Web sites were feasting on craigslist like parasites, cutting and pasting craigslist ads onto their sites, usually including a link to craigslist for direct access to the ad. Craigslist had finally had enough and demanded that the scrapers stop. Did it want to protect users from banner ads, or was it starting to become more conscious of protecting its profits?

Apache

Around the same time that David Garrison was touring France, talking to his investors about whether he was the president of the Internet, engineers all over the world were excitedly grappling with the new Web technology and its implications.

The first popular browser for surfing the Web came from the NCSA Project at the University of Illinois. Engineers had been working there for years developing the precursors and basic backbone of the Web. But when people started seeing the true potential of the Web—or, more accurately, the true profit potential—they left NCSA and started companies like Netscape, whose initial public offering is synonymous with the start of the Internet boom.

The departure of the engineers from NCSA left a need for other talented people to create the architecture of the Net. Engineers from all over the world would come up against a wall in their Web development, develop a patch to fix the problem, and send it in for free to NCSA. They didn't demand any sort of payment. Instead, they'd wait and expect accolades or insults for their work. But they got neither. Just silence. For whatever reason, maybe because it was too overwhelmed with such e-mails, NCSA never bothered to reply.

The engineers didn't get angry at NCSA and start attacking it; nor did they have aspirations to create a large Internet company and sell overinflated stock. No. They just wanted their patches to be integrated, making the Web more efficient.

With no response from NCSA headquarters, the engineers started talking to one another through an e-mail list about the Web. One of those engineers reflected, "Why not just do it ourselves?" He reasoned that if NCSA wasn't going to post the patches, they might as well do it. Another engineer, Brian Behlendorf, even had a name for the project, one whose profound implications he probably didn't know about. In his book *Rebel Code*, Glyn Moody explains how Behlendorf came up with the name "Apache." It came to him sort of out of the blue and intrigued him: it was "something that wasn't Web this or Spider that, or Arachnid, or any of the other metaphors being used."

Behlendorf donated his computer as a place where other engineers could post their patches. Apache didn't have a strategic plan on how to move forward. It was a lot more organic—engineers would contribute, and the good patches would be picked up by other users. No one had a set role; people would just help out in the best way they could.

Soon the Apache site was receiving more and more visitors. Moody explains that "because the Apache group was based entirely on volunteers spread across the world, most of whom had full time jobs running websites, for example, it was decided to employ an unusual model" for the organization. This model would make Geronimo proud.

There was a core team of about ten engineers who would develop patches and maintain the Apache list. On the periphery were countless other individuals who would contribute patches. No one was really in charge, and the best ideas were the ones that got used. It was just like the Nant'an: you follow someone—in this case, use their patch—because you respect their skills and you like the results you get, not because the boss told you to.

Apache collected so many patches for the NCSA Project that eventually it posted its own version. The software was completely open-source—anyone who wanted to could download it for free, and anyone could make alterations. If your patches improved the original software in any way, and if enough people liked them, they would eventually be integrated into the main program.

Engineers all over the world started using Apache to run their Web site servers. These weren't engineers who wanted to save money or techies who wanted to be experimental. Some very large organizations—such as MIT and Yahoo—adopted Apache code. Apache quickly developed from an alternative collection of patches to the industry standard.

There were other players as well—mainly Microsoft and Netscape—but neither company offered as compelling a product. Eventually, Apache gained the bulk of the industry's market share; today, 67 percent of all Web sites run on Apache.

Most of us don't even realize that when we surf the Web, we are constantly benefiting from the Apache patches that engineers have been donating for over a decade. Apache's most significant role was what it prevented: a fight between two huge spiders—

Microsoft, with its near-monopoly on operating systems, on one side of the ring, and Netscape, with plenty of cash from a successful public offering, on the other. The giants were poised for a fight between platforms—just like Mac and PC. If not for Apache, engineers would have had to make a decision to align with one of the giants, hoping their platform would win out in the end. For users, surfing a Web site would have been reminiscent of the old days of renting a movie. Rather than a clerk asking, "VHS or Beta?" a visitor to a site would have had to choose between Netscape and Microsoft platforms.

The Apache software is similar to other open-source projects such as Linux, the operating system that's like a free version of Microsoft Windows. In the face of open systems—where anyone can contribute and everyone can have the software for free—traditional spider organizations are finding that they have to adapt and become more starfishlike. If you're Microsoft, and all of a sudden your competitors are giving out better products for free, pretty soon you'll lose your competitive advantage. Later on we'll see how other big names like Sun and IBM have had to adapt. For now, it's enough to realize that just as the Apache Indians introduced a new way of fighting to the Spanish, so has the new Apache changed the software industry.

Wikipedia

We all remember doing school reports in the sixth grade. Back then, research meant going to the library and hoping that the *Encyclopaedia Britannica* wasn't checked out.

If you were doing a report on penguins, you'd take out the

"P" volume and pretty much copy word for word the entry on the bird. Then you'd slap on a hand-drawn illustration, slip the paper into a plastic cover, and you were done. The encyclopedia was the savior of lazy elementary school children everywhere.

When we heard about a new online encyclopedia, we expected a variation on *Britannica*—short articles written by experts, covering the basics on a variety of subjects. But then we found out that the entries were all user-contributed. A truly open model.

Wikipedia has fascinating origins that in many ways capture the evolution of an open system. It started with Jimmy Wales, a successful options-trader-turned-Internet-entrepreneur-turned-philanthropist. In 2000, Wales launched a free online encyclopedia to be used by children whose parents couldn't afford their own set. The project, called Nupedia, used peer review. But getting something published on Nupedia was a chore.

There were seven steps: assignment, finding a lead reviewer, lead review, open review, lead copyediting, open copyediting, and final approval and markup. It was a handful just to read these instructions, let alone execute them. The process was tedious; PhDs and other experts were assigned as authors. As the articles were slowly being churned out, Larry Sanger, Nupedia's editor-in-chief, learned about something called a wiki. Derived from the Hawaiian word for "quick," wiki is a technology that allows Web site users to easily (and quickly) edit the content of the site themselves.

Sanger pitched the idea of using wiki technology at Nupedia. Taking a cue from Bill W., Jimmy Wales agreed, and Wikipedia was born. Just like AA, the project took off. Within five years, Wikipedia was available in two hundred languages and had extensive articles—more than one million in the English-language section alone—on a host of topics. And just like the AA offshoots, Wikipedia spawned Wiktionary, Wikibooks, and Wikinews.

As for Nupedia, it managed to squeeze out twenty-four finalized articles and seventy-four articles still in progress before closing down. Larry Sanger's idea to introduce wiki technology ended up costing him his job—the users took over the editorial functions.

When we first visited the Wikipedia site, we thought it was a quaint idea but honestly had fairly low expectations about the quality of the articles, and we expected to find more vandalism than on a 1980s subway car. We were wrong on both counts.

First, the quality of the articles is outstanding—the vast majority are clearly written and succinct and have just the right level of depth. People take great care in making the articles objective, accurate, and easy to understand. This brings us to the seventh principle of decentralization: *put people into an open system and they'll automatically want to contribute.*

And not only do people contribute, their contributions are remarkably accurate. In fact, an investigation led by *Nature* magazine found that Wikipedia and the *Encyclopaedia Britannica* are almost equally accurate. "The average science entry in Wikipedia," concluded the experts, "contained around four inaccuracies; Britannica, about three." Like concerned and thoughtful neighbors, members of the Wikipedia community care enough to contribute regularly and are mindful to keep the content accurate.

During our initial search of Wikipedia, we wanted to do a test. Does it really cover everything? We typed in the first obscure reference we could think of—our favorite 1980s sitcom, *Three's Company.* Sure enough, there was the article. It was fairly complete, but the information on the show's landlords, Mr. and Mrs. Roper, was lacking. We read the article and decided to hit the "Edit" button—we were about to make our first contribution to the site. At first, it seemed a little weird—wow, we have the power to change this entry, and everyone in the world will see it (or at least *Three's Company* fans). But then again, every Wikipedia article is made up of contributions by ordinary users just like us.

The second page we visited was the entry for the group Environmental Defense. Finding the entry rather vague and inaccurate, Rod spent an hour writing a summary of the organization and its highlights. He cut and pasted his revisions from Microsoft Word and updated the article. What he created was definitely an improvement, but graphically, the different fonts and type sizes made the article look messy.

Because Wikipedia allows everyone to contribute, someone quickly came along to beautify Rod's work. This time it was Walt Lockley, who describes himself on his own page as "an architectural consultant and writer." His contributions to Wikipedia "concentrate on design issues. Product design, interior design, architecture." Lockley finds pages on Wikipedia that are, by his aesthetic standards, "in terrible shape" and cleans them up.

The very next day after Rod posted the Environmental Defense article, Walt came along and made it aesthetically pleasing. We've never met Walt, never even sent him an e-mail. But still he came along to contribute to the larger Wikipedia community, without insulting Rod's work and without ever demanding remuneration. Walt just wanted to help out. There's just something rewarding about contributing.

Today there are experts all over Wikipedia contributing in any and all ways—from providing up-to-the-minute information about a natural disaster to writing in-depth articles about the psychologist Carl Jung. This leads us to the second surprise we encountered—the vast majority of contributions are positive.

In fact, it took months of using Wikipedia before we encountered a vandal. This person added a reference on the Inca page claiming that *"the Inca empire proved that giant, man eating rats lived for up to one-hundred years."* Within nine hours, another user, Jessica, "an architect living on the Lower East Side in Manhattan," had removed the vandalism.

When we investigated craigslist, we learned that the site is a virtual neighborhood. The same can be said of Wikipedia. It remains a nice, clean neighborhood because people like Jessica remove vandalism as soon as they see it. The unnamed Inca vandal has continued to alter pages. Some of the vandal's hits include adding "max is a looser" in the chemistry article and "Y is yor cat eating my anal fluids with a fork :D" in the illegal drug trade entry. In each case, the vandalism was quickly cleaned up.

Members themselves take on the job of policing the site. There are some who even volunteer as Wikipedia cops—people like user Quadell, who describes himself as a "Wikipedia custodian." He says of his job, "I have keys to the mop room, and I mop things up." Being a custodian isn't an easy job. Quadell has an ongoing battle with vandals whose attacks on his own entry have included deleting all the text and replacing it with statements like: "It is kinda boring here in the middle of the night, so I thought to myself, maybe I should valdalize Quadell's page, he doesn't mind!" and "Quadell is an AssPirate!"

Wikipedia has the power to "lock" certain pages, either because of rampant vandalism or because a certain topic (say Islam) is controversial. The matter is then debated in the public forum until users agree on some sort of compromise, at which time the page is quickly unlocked. But Wikipedia always strives to keep pages open. Even Quadell's page—though regularly vandalized—remains open.

Burning Man

The Burning Man festival, which happens yearly in the Nevada desert, is known for eclectic costumes, rave music, and a host of naked people on Ecstasy and pot. It's also the only 24/7 decentralized experience you can find these days.

Because of its wild reputation, there's a certain embarrassment associated with going to Burning Man—if your coworkers ever tell you that they're taking "a weekend trip to the desert" just before Labor Day, chances are they're not telling you the whole truth. In reality, they're heading seventy miles north of Nowhere, Nevada, to a dry lakebed where over thirty thousand people congregate once a year.

Ori and his friends drove up in a beat-up Toyota, with their mountain bikes strapped to the back. They'd heard that bikes were the only good way of getting around Burning Man because it's too big to walk and conventional cars aren't allowed. They passed Reno and then made a left off Interstate 80 onto a two-lane highway that stretched across the desert. After they drove by an Indian reservation, there was nothing. Eventually there weren't even trees or shrubbery—just rocks and mountains. Farther still, in the distance, they saw a dry lakebed and a sea of tents and RVs. The glow of its flashing lights made it look almost like Vegas.

They arrived at Burning Man after dark and started looking for their friend Craig's camp (no, not the Craig with the list). RVs and tents form a temporary town called Black Rock City. The city is built around the "playa"—the dry lakebed. Streets are formed by concentric circles. This year they were named after planets. Radiating out from the playa, like bicycle spokes, are more streets named after the times of the day. So you might arrange to meet someone at, say, 10:30 and Venus.

They found Craig's camp at 2:00 and Uranus. Craig is a Dartmouth grad who lives in San Francisco with his wife. By day, he's a product manager at a software company, but he's also an intensely creative person—the kind of guy who turned his basement into a fully functional tiki bar. To entice his wife to come to Burning Man with him, Craig converted an old Ford Escort into a giraffe with a twenty-foot neck. She was so flattered that Craig had created the giraffe for her that she agreed to forgo clean sheets and showers for a week and came along.

Craig attached a few pieces of plywood to the roof of the car-turned-giraffe as a platform for up to twelve passengers. He operated the car from the roof as well, by attaching long PVC pipes to the brakes, the accelerator, and the steering wheel. He drove the car by pulling or rotating the appropriate pipe.

There are two main decentralized qualities to Burning Man. The first is that there really aren't many rules. If you'd like to dress up in a funky costume, go ahead. If you'd like to wear nothing at all, go ahead. If you'd like to build a twenty-foot giraffe and drive it across the desert, go ahead.

Craig's creation is called an "art car," for obvious reasons. There are lots of other art cars at Burning Man, including a school-bus-turned-disco, a pirate ship on wheels, a menacing shark, even a beat-up city-bus-turned-submarine. There are also art installations, like a homemade, hand-powered Ferris wheel. It takes a lot of trust to ride and a little bit of getting used to the fact that there's no one there to make you sign a release form.

The other thing that takes getting used to is that nothing costs money. That's the second decentralized quality of Burning Man—it's based on a gift economy. You provide things—from snow cones to hand-decorated T-shirts—because you want to, as a way to contribute to the community, not because you expect anything in return. The only things that you *can* pay for at Burning Man are ice and coffee. All proceeds from both go to support the local school district.

It's strange how quickly you get used to this gift economy. It's liberating to feel that nobody is trying to sell you anything. If you want their product, you can have it. If you don't, that's fine.

But Burning Man wasn't all about exchanging free gifts. One night at about two in the morning, Ori and a friend encountered a man attacking the street sign for Venus and 4:00. The first thought that went through their heads was, *Where are the cops?* But there weren't any cops. It was up to them.

The guy looked angry, so they approached him with caution. "Hi," they said. He looked at them, still pulling at the sign.

"Hi," they said again. Trying not to sound harsh, they added, "What are you doing?"

The man stopped his attack but still maintained a strong grip on the sign. "I don't know," he said with such sincerity that you had to believe him. "I just can't find my camp. I've been walking and walking around, and I'm just so frustrated." He started crying.

"It's going to be okay," they said.

"I don't know where my camp is. And I'm so frustrated. It's not what you think—I'm not trying to cause problems."

"Well, if you tear down this sign," they pointed out, "then no one will be able to find where they're going."

That logic seemed to work. He let go of the sign and agreed to let them help him find his camp.

For the next hour or so they walked through the solar system looking for this man's camp. They started with the inner planets. They exhausted Mercury and Venus and left Earth, still with no results. They finally found his camp somewhere near Jupiter and 7:00. Yes, he may have been on something, or maybe he was just dehydrated and sleep-deprived, or maybe there was something else going on. But he demonstrated something important—open systems can't rely on a police force. On the one hand, there's freedom to do what you want, but on the other hand, you have added responsibility: because there are no police walking around maintaining law and order, everyone becomes a guardian of sorts. You become responsible for your own welfare and that of those around you. In open systems, the concept of "neighbor" takes on more meaning than just the person next door.

That captures the Burning Man experience. When you put people in an open system, some of them will get high, dance all night long, and attack street signs. But most people will create elaborate art, share snow cones, and try as hard as they can—in their own way—to contribute to the community. And Burning Man, though outside the mainstream, holds a crucial lesson for businesses. When you give people freedom, you get chaos, but you also get incredible creativity. Because everyone tries to contribute to the community, you get a great variety of expression—everything from twenty-foot giraffes to seminars on raw food, to free haircuts, to a five-star hotel-tent.

CHAPTER 4

Standing on Five Legs

None of his fellow Londoners would've guessed that Granville Sharp—a skilled musician and accomplished attorney—was about to change the world. Nor did anyone suspect that a group of religious outsiders would hold unseen powers, or that a small AA-like group would change the laws of the greatest empire of the time.

As Adam Hochschild describes in his book *Bury the Chains*, it all started in 1765. Granville Sharp's life wasn't exactly ordinary—he played the clarinet, flute, oboe, kettle drums, and harp in a twelve-member family orchestra that often performed on a floating barge. Sharp wasn't really looking for a cause, but a cause found him in the form of Jonathan Strong, a sixteen-year-old slave who was nearly beaten to death by his master. But Strong survived and received medical help from Sharp's brother, who was a doctor.

Strong eventually healed and, with the help of Sharp and his brother, began making a better life for himself. But he was still considered his master's property. When the master found Strong two years later, now healthy and able to work, he attempted to reclaim the young man. Sharp was indignant at the injustice. How could Jonathan Strong, who had such a determination to live, such a will to make it, be considered mere property? He had to do something to help Strong and agreed to represent him in court. The case went down to the wire: Strong was about to be shipped to the Americas to be sold when Sharp succeeded in winning his freedom. The process changed Sharp forever. Soon more slaves were seeking his counsel, and he often found himself in court fighting for their rights. He became determined to abolish slavery.

Sharp's views put him in a tiny minority. Most people saw nothing wrong with slavery, a practice that was older than the Roman empire. Not only did people support slavery, but big industry was behind it as well. At the time, the sugar business was one of the biggest in the world; revenues from sugar production dwarfed those of most other industries. Sugar was huge, and it depended on slavery for its survival. When Sharp wrote pamphlets about the mistreatment of slaves aboard transport ships, Big Sugar declared that the journey was the happiest time in an African person's life. When abolitionists organized sugar boycotts, the industry warned people that *not* eating sugar was bad for your teeth. To say that Sharp had an uphill battle ahead of him is an understatement.

When Sharp started his campaign, he didn't have access to the powerful elite. His cause went against public sentiment, and he was going against big business interests. But he started a crusade nonetheless. He continued defending slaves' rights in court, wrote and distributed abolitionist literature, and talked about slavery to everyone he met.

After eighteen years, Sharp had made some progress on his campaigns, but things really started to take off when he turned to the Quakers. Now, in eighteenth-century London, the Quakers were viewed in the same way that the Hare Krishna are viewed today. They were a marginalized religion, often mocked for their peculiarities (like refusing to take their hats off when they greeted others and calling people "thou" instead of "you"). Unlike the Hare Krishna, however, the Quakers had always been nonhierarchical, shunning priests and other higher-ups. Quaker meetings began in silence, and whichever congregant was moved to do so spoke for as long as he or she wanted. They believed that all people have an "inner light" and should be treated as equals, and they were therefore staunch opponents of slavery. Although Sharp wasn't a Quaker himself, he joined a small Quaker group. It was organized as a circle, the first of five important foundations of a decentralized organization.

A decentralized organization stands on five legs. As with the starfish, it can lose a leg or two and still survive. But when you have all the legs working together, a decentralized organization can really take off.

LEG 1: Circles

Circles are important to nearly every decentralized organization we've explored. The Apaches, for example, lived in many small, nonhierarchical groups spread across the Southwest. Though they shared a common heritage and tradition, each group maintained its own particular habits and norms. Each Apache group resembled a circle: independent and autonomous.

But membership in an Apache circle was rather exclusive. The only way for outsiders to join a circle, in fact, was to be taken in battle. But once brought into a circle, members were accepted as Apache—whether by birth, adoption, or capture. That's the thing about circles: once you join, you're an equal. It's then up to you to contribute to the best of your ability.

In the days of the Apaches, communication between different communities was difficult, and sharing information took days or weeks. But the advent of telephones and cheap transportation has made communication virtually instantaneous. Until the Internet age, circles were confined to a physical location. People could join an AA circle, but in order to take part, they had to show up at a meeting. The Internet has allowed circles to become virtual: members join from their computers without ever leaving home.

The barrier to forming and joining virtual circles has become dramatically lower. Joining circles is so easy and seamless, in fact, that most of us, whether we realize it or not, are members of a decentralized circle of one kind or another. Take craigslist, for example. If you browse the ads, post one yourself, or contact a seller, you've just become a part of a virtual craigslist circle. It's not a close-knit group of people, but the sense of community and support is still there. The site has many circles, each based in a metropolitan community: there's a San Francisco craigslist, a New York craigslist, and so on.

Unlike Apache circles, anyone can join or contribute to organizations like Wikipedia. As they've become virtual, circles have also become more amorphous and difficult to identify. There aren't groups of Wikipedia users meeting together in rooms somewhere. Instead, a Wikipedia circle is made up of individuals contributing to a particular entry. Some members write the article, others edit it, still others beautify it. Membership becomes highly fluid. Unlike Apache circles, whose members lived together 24/7, virtual circles can be very fleeting. Because participants aren't spending every moment together, their bond isn't as strong. An Apache would do anything to protect a fellow tribe member—even risk life and limb. Members of craigslist aren't going to die for each other.

Virtual circles have also become much larger than those of, say, AA, where the size of the circle is limited by the number of people who can fit into a room. Now a circle can have a nearly unlimited number of participants. But there's a trade-off. On the one hand, it's easy to join, and with numbers you get diversity. On the other hand, when circles take on more than fourteen or so members, the bond breaks down. Members become more anonymous, and that opens the door to free-riding or destructive behavior. No longer does everyone have to pull their weight. Members of eMule can download songs all day long without ever contributing a single tune. Likewise, it's easier to vandalize Quadell's page on Wikipedia if you never have to meet him in person.

Circles gain freedom and flexibility when they go virtual, but there's a reason thousands of people travel all the way to the Nevada desert for a week once a year. Being in the physical presence of other participants adds a dimension of closeness, and a sense of ownership emerges. Members make Burning Man what it is, not some event production company. When you attend Burning Man, you become part of the organization. You own the experience and develop a sense of responsibility and belonging. That's why a virtual Burning Man isn't very appealing. Similarly, an AA circle depends on physical contact to keep members accountable to one another. When you see people face to face, it's harder to brush them off.

Because circles don't have hierarchy and structure, it's hard to maintain rules within them; no one really has the power to enforce them. But circles aren't lawless. Instead of rules, they depend on norms. AA has norms about confidentiality and support. Wikipedia has norms for editing entries. The Apache software has norms for developing code. Burning Man has norms for maintaining a gift economy. The norms, in fact, become the backbone of the circle. Because they realize that if they don't enforce the norms no one will, members enforce the norms with one another. In doing so, members begin to own and embrace the norms as their own. As a result of this self-enforcement, norms can be even more powerful than rules. Rules are someone else's idea of what you should do. If you break a rule, just don't get caught and you'll be okay. But with norms, it's about what you as a member have signed up for, and what you've created.

As the norms of a circle develop, and as members spend more time together, something fascinating happens: they begin to trust one another. Members of AA reveal their deepest thoughts and feelings, trusting that other members will keep the information safe and provide unconditional support. Though virtual circles have become more anonymous, they're still based on trust. Contributors to Wikipedia trust one another to edit their articles. Craigslist users feel that the site is a community and tend to put more faith in a fellow craigslist user than they would in a person off the street. Members assume the best of each other, and generally that's what they get in return.

They are also motivated to contribute to the best of their abilities. Users of eMule could easily be free-riders, but instead, most share their files with the whole world. Engineers post their content to Apache because they want to make the program better. Glenn passed along the free boxes to other craigslist members because he wanted to contribute. In a way, the fact that Wikipedia isn't overrun by vandals is testament to the fact that most people, given the chance, want to make a positive contribution. Maybe we're getting sentimental, but we can't help agreeing with Scott Cook, founder of Intuit, when he says, "Wikipedia proves that people are basically good."

LEG 2: The Catalyst

People like Granville Sharp, Bill W., and an Apache Nant'an are cast from a mold that is vastly different from that of a traditional executive. In a way, their leadership style resembles iron.

Here's what we mean. Take nitrogen and hydrogen, two of the most common elements on earth, put them in a container, close the lid, come back a day later, and . . . nothing will have happened. But add ordinary iron to the equation and you'll get ammonia, an important ingredient in fertilizers, polymers, and glass cleaners. The thing is, ammonia doesn't have any iron in it—it's made solely of hydrogen and nitrogen. The iron in this equation remains unchanged: it just facilitates the bonding of hydrogen and nitrogen in a certain way.

Iron is a catalyst. In chemistry, a catalyst is any element or compound that initiates a reaction without fusing into that reaction. In open organizations, a catalyst is the person who initiates a circle and then fades away into the background. In Apache circles, the Nant'an played the role of a catalyst. A Nant'an generated ideas and then allowed the circle to follow through. He could lead by example, but he never forced his views on others.

Likewise, Bill W. was the catalyst of AA. He started the organization but stepped aside when he saw that AA was taking off. Bill W. let go of the reins and allowed AA to become its own entity.

We see the same pattern with every decentralized organization: a catalyst gets a decentralized organization going and then cedes control to the members. Craig Newmark lets the users of craigslist decide which categories to list on the site. Jimmy Wales allows the members to take over the content of Wikipedia. Brian Behlendorf contributes his computer and lets the programmers take control of the Apache server program. The creator of eMule is the ultimate catalyst. No one knows who he or she is, and he or she has certainly ceded control: the source code for the program is right there for anyone to use. If, instead of giving the software away, the eMule catalyst had stuck around and tried to capitalize on the program, eMule would have been sued out of existence.

In a way, the difference between traditional leaders and catalysts is like the difference between Julie Andrews's characters in *The Sound of Music* and *Mary Poppins*. In *The Sound of Music*, Maria enters a dysfunctional family, teaches the children a valuable lesson, convinces the father to pay attention to his kids, and shows the family how to get along. Likewise, Mary Poppins visits an equally (albeit charmingly) dysfunctional family, gets equally adorable children to behave, urges equally clueless parents to pay attention to their kids, finds equally effective ways for everyone to get along, and sings equally catchy tunes.

At the end of *The Sound of Music*, though, Maria, after falling in love with the children and the father, sticks around. It's obvious that from now on she'll be the one running the show. Mary Poppins, on the other hand, chim-chim-in-eys right out of London. It's not that Mary Poppins has a fear of commitment. From the very beginning, it's clear that she's come to do a job. Her job is complete when the family can thrive on its own. Once she accomplishes her goal, she rides her umbrella into the sunset.

In letting go of the leadership role, the catalyst transfers ownership and responsibility to the circle. Without Mary Poppins, the family takes responsibility for itself. A catalyst isn't usually in it for praise and accolades. When his or her job is done, a catalyst knows it's time to move on.

Once the catalyst leaves, however, his or her presence is still felt. The catalyst is an inspirational figure who spurs others to action. Circles don't form on their own. Put a bunch of people in the same room together, and they might talk about the weather in random groups of twos and threes. Add a catalyst, and soon they'll be sitting around in a circle discussing their shared love of skiing or antique lampshades. A catalyst develops an idea, shares it with others, and leads by example.

A catalyst is like the architect of a house: he's essential to the long-term structural integrity, but he doesn't move in. In fact, when the catalyst stays around too long and becomes absorbed in his creation, the whole structure becomes more centralized. Craig Newmark of craigslist was in this predicament. He built a great site, but how much did craigslist still need him? If you owned a multimillion-dollar company, you'd much rather be Maria and stick around than fly off like Mary Poppins.

Although Sharp didn't leave the abolitionist movement, he most definitely gave circles their freedom. He wasn't interested in creating an empire under his control; he was focused on sparking a movement to end slavery. It was in letting go that Sharp enabled abolitionist circles to proliferate.

LEG 3: Ideology

What makes members join a circle? Why spend the time and make the effort to participate? As we've seen, there usually isn't much money to be made in decentralized organizations.

Open systems offer a sense of community, but so do lots of other organizations. Microsoft employees have a sense of community—they share a common bond and friendships—but they also get paid to collaborate. The engineers at Apache don't get paid a penny. They're motivated by a desire to create a better product. They believe in an open system and respect one another's contributions—not because they have to but because they want to. Yes, many open systems, such as Wikipedia, offer services for free. But people could easily use the library or a search engine to retrieve similar information. Yet people not only gravitate to Wikipedia but also regularly contribute.

It's not just about community, not just about getting stuff for free, not just about freedom and trust. Ideology is the glue that holds decentralized organizations together. The Apaches held a common belief that they belonged on the land and deserved to be self-governing. Those few Apaches who didn't hold this ideology accepted the Spanish invitation to become farmers and integrate into a centralized system. But those who stayed with the tribe held firmly to the notion of independence. Anyone who interfered with that ideology—whether a Spaniard, a Mexican, or an American—became the enemy. The Apaches held to their ideology so strongly that they were willing to fight and sacrifice themselves for their cause. Without the ideology, the Apaches wouldn't have had the motivation to remain decentralized.

At AA, the ideology is that people can help each other out of addiction. The twelve steps reflect the implications of this ideology. People who don't buy into the twelve steps aren't likely to stay in AA. But those who do follow the twelve steps do so rigorously. They believe that if they are ever tempted to ignore the ideology, they will revert to alcoholism. Likewise, for Sharp and the Quakers, fighting slavery was such a strong motivator that many dedicated their entire lives to the cause.

Starfish organizations spawned by the Internet may have less meaningful ideologies. Take eMule, with its ideology that exchanging free music is worthwhile. Millions might subscribe to that ideology, but no one would dedicate their life to it. Same thing with craigslist and Wikipedia. Their respective ideologies (that posting to a community or collaborating on articles is worthwhile) are not nearly as powerful as those held by the Apaches or AA.

That's why we wouldn't count on eMule, craigslist, or Wikipedia necessarily being around forever. It's easy enough for another player to come around and offer a similar ideology. But we can expect AA and its offshoots to be around as long as there's addiction.

LEG 4: The Preexisting Network

The Quakers had little political power or influence and were a marginalized group. But their marginalization ultimately gave the Quakers a different kind of power. Because they were outsiders, they were forced to form their own culture, business relationships, and community. Here was a robust network of people who lived together, conducted business with one another, and shared a common belief system. Put together a close-knit community with shared values and add a belief that everyone's equal, and what do you get? Decentralization. The Quakers weren't just decentralized themselves: they served as the decentralized platform upon which the antislavery movement was built. This piggybacking effect enabled the abolitionist movement to take off.

The Quakers had over twenty thousand members in England alone. They were already well versed in working together in circles and shared a common ideology. For eighteen years, Sharp went around England trying to win over the public and the courts. But without an army, the effort was quixotic. It was too difficult to build a brand-new decentralized organization, especially with the vast majority of people supporting slavery. But the Quakers gave the movement a platform.

Almost every decentralized organization that has made it big was launched from a preexisting platform. Bill W., the founder of AA, drew upon the Oxford Group, an independent Christian movement started by a renegade Lutheran minister. The Oxford Group had established circles and even a six-step program for recovery. Bill W. changed the six steps into twelve, borrowed the methodology, and launched his first AA circle.

But gaining entrance into a preexisting network isn't as simple as just showing up with a good idea. It might have been easier for Sharp if the Quakers had been centralized. He could have met with the leaders and convinced them to mobilize their followers and engage them in antislavery campaigns. But centralized organizations aren't good platforms. For one thing, if orders come from above, the membership might follow, but they won't be inspired to give it their all. Second, leaders in top-down organizations want to control what's happening, thereby limiting creativity. Third, and most important, centralized organizations aren't set up to launch decentralized movements. Without circles, there isn't the infrastructure for people to get involved and take ownership of an idea.

Decentralized networks, however, provide circles and an empowered membership and typically have a higher tolerance for innovation. But without a person in charge, Sharp had to rely on personal connections with the members. Though not a Quaker himself, Sharp didn't judge the Quakers, nor did he force his ideas on them. Instead, he slowly gained their trust and friendship.

Typically, it takes the special skills of a catalyst like Sharp to enter a network. But the Internet, as we've seen, changed everything. In Sharp's day, decentralized organizations were a rarity and entrance into them was difficult, but today the Internet serves as an open platform on the back of which a wide variety of starfish organizations can be launched. The Internet is a breeding ground and launching pad for new starfish organizations. Skype, eMule, and craigslist are among the many decentralized organizations that have been launched atop the Internet.

The implications of the Internet for decentralization are profound. For centuries, people would start decentralized organizations, but because a platform like the Quakers was a rarity, these organizations remained both scarce and largely social—as opposed to profit-driven. The Internet not only makes it easier for people to communicate but provides a fertile ground for a host of new decentralized organizations. It is because of the Internet and the platform it provides that we're seeing a revolution.

Even with the help of the Quaker platform, Sharp could not have completely abolished slavery without the fifth leg. Though he was a passionate catalyst, Sharp needed another person to execute on the vision. Someone like Thomas Clarkson.

LEG 5: The Champion

In 1785 Thomas Clarkson entered an abolitionist essay contest. His main motivation was to win the prize, but in researching the topic, he was more and more bothered by what he learned: how abhorrent the conditions were aboard transport ships and how masters dehumanized and mistreated their so-called property.

Clarkson began to sympathize with the abolitionist ideology. After he won the contest, he developed the zeal and drive to actively fight slavery. Clarkson met Sharp, and the two hit it off. If Sharp was the visionary, Clarkson was the implementer. Clarkson was what we call the "champion."

A champion is relentless in promoting a new idea. Catalysts are charismatic, but champions take it to the next level. A catalyst's charisma, like that of the Nant'ans, has a subtlety to it. Catalysts inspire and naturally connect people, but there's nothing subtle about the champion. Just ask the folks at the Berkeley post office in California—they're still talking about Leor Jacobi.

If anyone personifies the champion, it's Leor. He's always been a natural people person and an even better salesman. As a small child, when he'd go out with his parents to a restaurant, he'd leave the table and engage the other diners in conversation. He couldn't help it. You'd think that while people might have found this cute at first, the cuteness quickly would have become an invasion of personal space. Not with Leor. Even at that age, Leor was able to draw people in. They were fascinated by him.

Leor has always been naturally passionate and lively; when he becomes intrigued with an idea, his bite resembles that of a Rottweiler—he'll never let go. When he learned to play chess, he wouldn't stop until he was one of the best players in the state. When he got into music, he formed a successful band. But when he became a vegan (a vegetarian who doesn't drink milk or eat eggs), he found something to really sink his teeth into.

Most people who become vegetarian change their eating habits, start shopping at Whole Foods, and maybe slap a bumper sticker on their car. But when Leor got excited about being a vegan, everyone knew about it. He couldn't do anything halfway. He started organizing events, attending conferences, and engaging nearly everyone he met in conversation. Even when he called the 411 operator, he'd end up talking about a vegan diet. Something about the way Leor spoke—his excitement or his charm—made everyone feel comfortable with him and interested in what he had to say. The phone operator, for example, spent an hour talking to him and decided to give the new diet a try.

Likewise, when Leor went to mail a letter, he befriended each and every postal employee—even the folks who worked in the back. Remember, these aren't activists, these are postal employees, people who don't typically get excited about things and don't easily crack a smile. But when Leor came to the post office, they'd greet him like a long-lost friend. Nearly everyone had that reaction to Leor, and within a year of starting to promote a vegan diet, he had launched a national organization, established a vegan Web site, secured vegan meal options at college dining halls across the country, helped open a chain of vegetarian restaurants, and obtained coverage on major TV networks and in newspapers. And just for good measure, he won a trademark dispute with McDonald's Corporation.

It was just this kind of energy that Clarkson brought to the abolitionist movement. Clarkson and Sharp formed a twelve-man circle in which they were two of three non-Quakers. The circle was completely flat; all decisions were made by consensus. Circle members soon began mobilizing other Quakers into action.

Champions are inherently hyperactive. Like catalysts, they operate well in nonhierarchical environments, but they tend to be more like salesmen than organizers or connectors. Selling is what

Clarkson did. He was the only member of the circle who worked on the issue full-time. He spent sixteen-hour days on the cause and traveled up and down the British Isles. For the next sixty years, Clarkson dedicated his life to the movement. He collected evidence from twenty thousand seamen. He participated in public debates, published newsletters, and made buttons. He met with opinion-makers, who respected him because he wasn't a Quaker. He even lobbied Parliament.

Whenever he entered a new town, Clarkson helped form an abolitionist circle. The network was gaining strength. As people learned about Clarkson's message, slavery became a hot topic. Slowly, he started winning over the hearts and minds of the public.

In 1833, years before its abolition in America, slavery was outlawed in England. Although Sharp was the catalyst of the movement—or rather, *because* he was a catalyst—he has remained absent from most history texts. Clarkson was soon forgotten as well.

Credit for the abolition of slavery was attributed to William Wilberforce, a politician who was the movement's ally and spokesman in Parliament. When Wilberforce died, his sons glorified him while bashing Clarkson. The leaders of the decentralized movement never bothered securing recognition for themselves, and failing to understand the power of a starfish organization, people credited the success of the movement to a politician.

The Five Legs in Action

The English abolitionist movement, having achieved its goals, eventually faded away, but not before it gave rise to another powerful force. Enter Elizabeth Cady Stanton, who was born in 1815 and grew up in New York, the daughter of a prominent judge. After the death of her brother, Stanton's father let her know of his disappointment at being left with a daughter. She was determined to accomplish everything he had and more. She learned Greek, entered literary contests, and participated in sports—all uncommon pursuits for women at the time.

At twenty-five, she married an abolitionist. Her husband introduced her to many key figures of the abolitionist movement, including Thomas Clarkson, the champion. "Having read of all these people," Stanton recalled, "it was difficult to realize as I visited them in their homes from day to day, that they were the same persons I had so long worshiped from afar!"

But her experience with the abolitionists wasn't all positive. When Stanton attended an antislavery convention, she was forced to sit in a segregated, screened-off section reserved for women. What was more, women were not allowed to speak or vote in the meeting. How can we fight for slaves' rights, she fumed, while denying women equal rights? Through her conversations with other women at the convention, Stanton entertained, for the very first time in her life, the notion of "the equality of the sexes."

Like Sharp, Stanton was a catalyst who, when presented with an ideology, catalyzed a new movement. For ten years, the idea of equal rights for women continued to percolate and grow in Stanton's mind. Nearly a decade later, events in her life made her feel that "all the elements had conspired to impel me to some onward step." She had to do something about women's rights. Repeating history half a world away, whom did Stanton hook up with but the preexisting network of the Quakers?

Taking a cue from the abolitionists, Stanton and the Quakers organized a women's rights convention, where Stanton suggested that women be allowed to vote. "If I had had the slightest premonition of all that was to follow that convention, I fear I should not have had the courage to risk it," Stanton later recalled. In the months and years that followed, every respected newspaper in the nation blasted Stanton. "All the journalists," she wrote, "from Maine to Texas, seemed to strive with each other to see which could make our movement the most ridiculous."

All the newspapers, that is, except the antislavery papers. Soon abolitionists began supporting this new ideology. Just as the abolitionist movement had piggybacked atop the Quaker network in England, the women's suffrage movement now piggybacked atop the abolitionist movement in the United States. Women's suffrage circles began forming all over the country.

But just as access to a preexisting network wasn't sufficient for Sharp, gaining access to the abolitionist movement wasn't enough to catapult Stanton's movement to success. She needed a Thomas Clarkson or a Leor Jacobi; when she met one three years later, everything changed. "How well I remember the day!" Stanton wrote. "There she stood, with her good, earnest face and genial smile . . . the perfection of neatness and sobriety. I liked her thoroughly, and why I did not at once invite her home with me to dinner, I do not know."

Stanton, the catalyst, had met her champion, Susan B. Anthony. The two hit it off from the start and became lifelong friends. While Stanton, the quintessential catalyst, kept pursuing new ways to expand women's rights, like winning women the right to divorce, Anthony, being the quintessential champion, stayed the course, relentlessly pursuing women's suffrage. She traveled all over the country, to the point where she had the train schedules memorized. She spoke in front of any group that was willing to listen, in churches, schoolhouses, halls, and barns. In short, she dedicated her life to the cause.

Stanton was amazed by Anthony's drive: "Holding public debates in some town with half-fledged editors and clergymen; next, sailing up the Columbia River and, in hot haste to meet some appointment, jolting over the rough mountains of Oregon and Washington; and then, before legislative assemblies, constitutional conventions, and congressional committees, discussing with senators and judges the letter and spirit of constitutional law." Like Clarkson, Anthony was always ready to speak on the subject she was so passionate about. This was in stark contrast to Stanton, who was much more reticent. For example, when the two visited an institute for the deaf in Michigan, Stanton was relieved: "There's one comfort in visiting this place; we shall not be asked to speak." But Anthony was bold and eagerly went up to the podium: "By the laughter, tears, and applause, the [deaf] pupils showed that they fully appreciated the pathos, humor, and argument."

Anthony was as brazen as she was bold. Although it was illegal for women to vote at the time, Anthony went to a polling place in Rochester, New York, and demanded to cast her ballot. When the clerk tried to explain that she couldn't, she threatened to sue him and eventually got her way. When she was arrested for having voted, she embraced the challenge. She spoke in every town in the county where she was to be tried, attracting massive crowds and successfully convincing them to support her cause. She talked to so many people, in fact, that the trial had to be moved to a different county. But the same thing happened there, and in several subsequent counties. Eventually, though, Anthony was tried and convicted, and the judge imposed a $100 fine. "May it please your honor," she told him, "I will never pay a dollar of your unjust penalty." She never did.

Anthony was willing to fight to the end. This passion and determination landed Susan B. Anthony's face on the dollar coin, while Elizabeth Cady Stanton took a backseat in the history books.

Stanton was the architect of a movement that changed the lives of American women. By creating circles, tapping into an ideology whose time had come, drawing upon a pre-existing network, and joining forces with a champion, Stanton changed the course of history in the most Mary Poppins of ways. She set the events in action, inspired a movement, and then let go.

CHAPTER 5

The Hidden Power

of the Catalyst

At first glance, Auren Hoffman and Josh Sage seem like complete opposites. Auren is what Jewish grandmothers call a *macher*, a wheeler and dealer. He's always involved in one venture or another. In college, it was student politics. During the dot-com era, it was a successful technology company. And so on. Auren looks and acts the part of the business guy. He's a fast talker and an even faster thinker. This quick thinking is combined with the kind of charisma usually reserved for seasoned senators and Fortune 500 CEOs. In earlier times, Auren would have been that neighborhood guy you go to when you need something done. His clothes are always sharp. His professionalism seems to radiate from his core. Posing for photos with Fortune

500 CEOs and world leaders, Auren looks comfortable and at ease—like he just belongs in the picture.

While Auren is having his picture taken with presidents, Josh Sage is hanging out with the likes of actor-activist Woody Harrelson. Though not a California native, Josh most definitely looks the part. He has a casual air and easygoing personality that is rarely encountered outside of northern California. Josh is deeply committed to social equality and to protecting the environment. He is friends with some of the country's leading activists and believes strongly in giving youth a voice.

When you get to know Auren and Josh, you learn that they have more in common than you'd initially think: both are catalysts. Whenever we've encountered a catalyst, we have found ourselves drawn in. It's hard not to be. They're just so different from most of us. But what is it specifically that makes them unique? What differentiates them? What are the qualities that make catalysts essential to the very creation of a decentralized organization?

We set out to understand the modern catalyst—one of the five legs of decentralization that is integral to any open system. What we discovered initially was interesting. But as we spent more time with the catalysts, powerful patterns emerged that weren't just new and interesting but also surprising. We were dealing with an entirely different creature from the CEO. In a way, we felt like Tom Nevins, the anthropologist, as he studied a completely different society and culture.

One of the most intriguing catalysts around is Jimmy Wales, the catalyst behind Wikipedia. In our conversation, Jimmy was warm and positive from the get-go. "I'm a pathologically optimistic person," he declared, adding, "I talk a lot about love and respect. Our community's core values are to be thoughtful and kind and to have no personal attacks. It's an ongoing process of making sure that people are happy doing what they're doing." When most people tell you something like that, you take it with a grain of salt. But when Jimmy told us about his values, we had no doubt that he was genuine. You trust him because you know that he trusts you.

In Jimmy's case, a big part of trusting people is relying on them to effectively build the site. "I couldn't write an encyclopedia by myself," he told us. "From the very beginning, Wikipedia was a community." As we continued our conversation, now-familiar themes emerged. "The main thing about Nupedia [the precursor to Wikipedia] was that it was a failure. Essentially, the design of Nupedia was very top-down, in the sense that there were seven-stage review processes, committees for this thing and the other, and basically very, very little work actually ever got done. Of course, I always say that, yes, Nupedia was a failed model, but the one thing it did do for us was create a strong community that got Wikipedia off to a good, strong start."

As a catalyst, it's all about letting go and trusting the community. For example, we asked Jimmy who's in charge of managing the server software for Wikipedia's computer system. "I have no idea," he said. "The users decide amongst themselves. I have no idea how they do it. It's just general consensus in the community who gets an account. And they watch each other." It was that simple.

Jimmy focuses a great deal of attention on maintaining the health of the Wikipedia community. "I go to speaking engagements all over the world at conferences, and everywhere I go I meet Wikipedia volunteers," he told us. "Usually we go off to dinner and talk shop about Wikipedia. The Wikipedia gossip is the same all over the world—just the characters are different. The problems that affect community are always the same problems." When he doesn't meet the members in person, Jimmy spends "a ton of time writing e-mails internally, to the community, touching base with people, discussing issues that come up on the mailing list." But "as far as working with Wikipedia, I don't write articles. Very, very little do I ever edit. But I do engage with people on policy matters and try to settle disputes."

That's pretty much the role Jimmy takes. He gives the community an incredible level of freedom. "There's no schedule, there's no direction for these people at all. Nobody's the boss of anybody. People just pick up projects and work on them. They remotely log into servers to work on them when they need maintenance. They reconfigure the networks when they need reconfiguring. It's all done completely willy-nilly, I mean with no organization at all. And yes, it works. Our site is sometimes slow, but the reason it's slow is we haven't bought enough hardware. We spend virtually all the money that we get just buying hardware. But it works."

Jimmy makes it work because he empowers people and gets out of the way. This theme emerged with every catalyst we met. Deborah Alvarez-Rodriguez is the head of Goodwill Industries of San Francisco. Like Jimmy, Deborah exudes warmth. She has a maternal quality to her, but at the same time, she isn't smothering. She recalled how she struck this balance when she was the director of San Francisco's Department of Children, Youth, and Their Families. The position was full of potential power, influence, and authority, none of which Deborah wanted. Like

Jimmy, Deborah started "thinking about, how do I help, how do I become more of a catalyst and let the young people and parents become more of a driving force in how change happens."

Deborah had a crazy idea: take all the advocacy groups that were normally a thorn in the city's side and open her office doors to them, inviting them in. "They'd start having places in my office to meet. And so the agency became this hub of activity." Working side by side, people began to trust each other.

To further facilitate trust and bonding, Deborah focused on ideology. She'd refuse to talk to organizations about concrete strategy and nuts and bolts. She'd tell them, "I'm not going to talk about programs or budgets. I'm not going to talk about any of that right now." Instead, she asked the groups about "what keeps you up at night, what brings joy—tears of joy in your eyes. And I'll share that with you as well. I want to understand you as a person." A catalyst's most important relationships are based on trust and understanding. Deborah "just knew that values were a stronger binding force than authority." These conversations were difficult at first. "It was a little bit scary for everybody. It was a little bit scary for me. It required me to have a certain amount of vulnerability as a leader."

But Deborah wasn't running a support group. She was dealing with passionate activist groups. How could she have these conversations with groups that might talk to her one day but, if they disagreed with her actions the next day, would burn her effigy on the steps of city hall? Surprisingly, Deborah welcomed the burning. "I will trust the authenticity of this relationship," she told the advocacy groups, "when I bring an idea and you guys look at me and say, 'That is absolutely the most idiotic idea

I have ever heard. What is wrong with you?' As long as you think everything I do smells like roses, we've got a problem."

Deborah was pleased when "it got to a point where they'd give me advance notice. They'd tell me, 'We're going to city hall, and we're going to burn your effigy on the steps.' So I'd say, 'Okay, what did I do this time?' When they'd explain, I'd say, 'You're right, I did all those things, and if they're upsetting you to that extent, then go for it, burn the effigy, and I appreciate the call.' Well, we had gotten to that point, you know, where we could do that with each other. There was enough respect to be able to do that." Imagine having so much faith and trust in a community that you'd continue talking to them, let alone respecting them, after they'd burned your effigy.

This kind of trust can yield powerful results. Deborah was able to make San Francisco the first city in the country to offer comprehensive health care to all children under the age of eighteen. But just as Deborah was reaching the peak of her success, she got "concerned that I would take on the persona of the charismatic leader and would overwhelm the policies and systems we designed. When it starts becoming more about me and less about what's happening, then we're walking a dangerous path." Deborah took a cue from Mary Poppins and left.

She eventually took a job as the CEO of Goodwill Industries of San Francisco, an organization, she realized, that needed to get back in touch with its ideology. Deborah is now busy starting circles, inviting participants from all levels of the company, and empowering them to take on important corporate decisions.

Keeping to her catalyst roots, Deborah refuses to be seen as the head. You'd be hard-pressed, in fact, to find her name on Goodwill's Web site. She knows that, in the words of the ancient Chinese philosopher Lao-tzu, "a leader is best when people barely know that he exists; not so good when people obey and acclaim him; worst when they despise him."

Not all catalysts are hidden. Auren Hoffman, in fact, is hard to miss. It's easy enough to find him on his Web site, and Auren isn't shy about getting his name out there. But Auren isn't all about Auren. For him, it's all about making connections. When Ori talked to Auren, for example, Auren quickly blurted out: "Hey, I know your friend Sara!" He'd met her at a conference, and Sara had asked him where he went to college. When he told her, Sara made the connection that Auren had gone to school with Ori. Although Sara was the one who identified the link, Auren stored the connection in his mind and saved it for the next time he and Ori talked. It's just how his mind works; he makes connections and likes putting people together. Auren is a compulsive connector, in fact. Just as an artist can't help but paint, Auren can't help but meet new people. "There are some people who believe in only having deep relationships with people," he said, "but then you're limited to twenty close friends. Beyond those twenty, every other relationship is a weaker tie. I find a lot of value in those weak ties."

Casual acquaintances fascinate him: "You can learn a lot, and you can meet really interesting people. Everyone's interesting for at least an hour. And most people remain interesting well beyond that." It comes so naturally to him that Auren figured out a way of capitalizing on his compulsion.

Like a good catalyst, Auren has launched a variety of networks. The Silicon Forum is a network of leading thinkers and business executives that convenes to discuss social issues; the CIO Symposium holds regular conference calls in which chief information officers from top companies share issues of importance to them; the Silicon Valley 100 enables marketers to get their products in the hands of the "biggest influencers in the San Francisco Bay Area." Auren's most interesting role, however, is as a catalyst-for-hire. His firm, Stonebrick, allows companies to create and draw upon decentralized networks. "Sometimes I can't believe people actually pay me for this," he said when describing his work. "The basic idea behind Stonebrick is to help companies find either customers or partners and help them build long-term relationships."

Companies hire Auren because he's able to navigate complex social networks. Auren constantly maps relationships in a way that is nearly impossible for most people. "A lot of people that you want to meet are not direct revenue relationships," he explained. "You might want to meet someone who's not necessarily a customer, say, but who might introduce you to customers. Or it could be someone who becomes a customer three or four years down the road."

For Auren, making introductions is intuitive. If most of us started thinking about all the people we know, trying to figure out who might benefit from knowing whom and how we could introduce them, we'd quickly get a headache. But for Auren, it comes naturally: "The thing I do when I meet someone is make a map: you went to school at Berkeley, so . . . you must know so-and-so. I always make that map every time I meet somebody." It takes a specialist like Auren to not only map people but use the map to make strategic introductions between the right individuals. He described a typical scenario: "So I say, 'Bob, you should meet Jane. You should grab lunch. You should meet up.' Before I do that, I'll check in with Jane: 'Jane, are you interested in an introduction to Bob's company?' " What's amazing is that everyone involved in the interaction ends up being grateful to Auren. If he does his job right, Bob benefits from meeting Jane; Jane, in turn, will have gained from meeting Bob. Auren makes the introductions, helps people connect, and then, in typical catalyst fashion, gets out of the way.

He also never works on commission. Why? "For a few reasons. First, it's a lot easier to be more ethically pure, and most of these people I'm introducing my customers to are people I know, people I like. And I think it would be weird if I actually benefited from that arrangement. The second reason why I don't take commission is that a lot of these introductions I make are much more long-term. So some of them are direct revenues that are going to happen, let's say, in the next few months. But some of these introductions will then yield further introductions. So they're influencers. And sometimes my customer is already talking to the client. And the other thing is that you never want to be in competition with the salesperson. So that would mean I'd be taking commission out of that salesperson's hands. Whereas in my job now I'm the salesperson's best friend."

Ironically, Auren doesn't consider himself a networker—at least not in the classic sense. "Networking is like, I want to meet person X, and I go network in to that person and find a way to meet them. But I like chaos. I never try to meet anybody. In fact, I much prefer meeting people . . . you know, if you think of a ladder, like a social ladder, I much prefer meeting people lower on the ladder than above me because I can help them more. It's fun to help people."

The thing about Auren is that he is genuinely interested in helping people. "It does take a certain personality," he said of the catalyst, "someone who likes to help people. Lots of people just know a lot of people." A catalyst, on the other hand, is "someone who every time they have a conversation with someone they're actively thinking, *How can I help this person? Who can I introduce this person to? I just want to help this person, I just want to make this person better.* People really, really want to help other people. And that's the most underutilized tool there is." Auren doesn't get paid for the vast majority of the connections he makes, and he certainly doesn't have an internal balance sheet reflecting whom he's helped and who owes him one.

This is where Auren and Josh Sage have a lot in common. Both have a passion for helping others. Josh doesn't connect businesses; he connects activists around the country. Josh has a passion about him that's contagious. He could be talking to you about something you know little about, and about which you care even less. Fifteen minutes later, though, you'll think it's the most important thing in the world, and you may very well ask Josh how you can get involved.

After the WTO protests in Seattle, Josh got together a group of activists, borrowed a beat-up RV, and went on the road, going from town to town creating circles to work on issues of globalization.

He understood that the way to mobilize people was by sharing inspirational stories. From there, the pattern is familiar. The activists shared a common ideology and created circles, which morphed into other circles around the world.

In addition to determination, it also requires a certain chutzpah to come into a new town in a beat-up RV and organize people. This combination of passion and chutzpah has made Josh a force to be reckoned with. He told us the story, for example, of how he decided to make a documentary about youth activism. While living in a van parked across the street from an editing studio so he could finish the film, he got in touch with Michael Stipe, the lead singer of the band REM, and persuaded him to show the film to MTV; then Josh negotiated with MTV to air the film in its entirety, completely unedited. It wasn't that MTV was desperate for programming, or that it couldn't find another video about environmentalism. It was that Josh's passion was contagious—it came across in his material. On top of that, he had the chutzpah to hold his ground.

Most of us couldn't imagine finding a way to connect into MTV, let alone convincing the network to air our homemade video. But catalysts have a mysterious way of getting things done.

David Martin, for example, is a real-estate mogul, a mover and shaker, and in every way looks the part of a successful CEO. On top of that, David is head of the Young Presidents' Organization (YPO), a CEO network with about 9,500 members around the world. His mannerisms, his southern accent, and his white hair and neatly trimmed beard make him look like he stepped out of an episode of *Dallas*. Even J. R. Ewing would have given David the respect he deserved.

David spends a big chunk of his time on the road. He meets with CEOs around the world and operates as a smooth and polished catalyst. He's always on the lookout for a champion, someone who can run with the ball. Like Deborah Alvarez-Rodriguez of

Goodwill, David is full of new ideas. He's a master at pitching the big idea, getting someone interested and bought in.

Though full of ideas, David is also a great listener. He realizes how important it is to understand what people truly want. He'll listen to you and find out what you're excited about, then suggest ways to channel that energy into a project. He'll guide you in putting your energy behind an effort, and only after you're fully engaged, spending all of your free time on it, will you pause and ask, "Hey, how did I end up running this project?" By then, David's job is done.

The Catalyst's Tools

It was in thinking about David Martin that it dawned on us: all of the catalysts we spoke to draw upon similar tools. And while no one can wake up one day and decide to become Auren Hoffman, we can certainly incorporate the tools of his trade.

Genuine Interest in Others To a catalyst, people are like walking novels. Information that most of us barely listen to is pure gold to someone like Auren. To understand this, think of the most boring person you've ever met. At a party, for example, someone might drone on about their days at this company or the other, and most people would nod their heads, put on a fake smile, and think about what they ate for dinner three nights ago. In all likelihood, whether consciously or unconsciously, the speaker picks up on this lack of interest and either tries to find another topic or turns silent. This is the cause of awkwardness in casual social situations. We talk to people we don't really know about stuff that we don't really care about, and it creates a sense of unease.

But chances are, if you talked to Auren, you wouldn't be able to have a boring conversation if you tried. That's because Auren is genuinely interested in others. In fact, Auren believes that if you find someone boring it's only because you, the listener, haven't asked the right questions or found that person's true passions.

We can tell when someone like Auren really cares about what we're talking about; when that happens, we tend to open up and reveal more about ourselves. The conversation naturally becomes more interesting, and we feel he has really been able to "get" us. It's at that point, when we feel understood, that we are most open to something new. We become willing to change.

This is the catalyst's essential tool. If you met Auren at a party and he called you a week later to introduce you to one of his friends, you'd be more likely to take his call and follow through than you would be if the call came from someone with whom you'd had a boring, artificial conversation.

Loose Connections Most of us have interesting personal conversations with a select group of our closest friends. But a catalyst is able to have these kinds of interactions with thousands—in fact, they thrive on meeting new people every day. It's impossible for someone like Jimmy Wales to have a deep relationship with each and every Wikipedia user he meets; there aren't enough hours in the day. For most of us, these casual interactions would get tiresome very quickly, and we'd yearn to spend time with our old friends. But because they are genuinely interested in others, catalysts find these kinds of relationships incredibly meaningful.

That's not to say that a catalyst can't have close personal friends. It's just that in addition to close friends, catalysts have a host of acquaintances. Knowing so many people allows a catalyst to make connections between individuals who would otherwise never meet.

Mapping While you're talking to Auren at a party, he won't just be intrigued by your stories, he'll also be mapping out how you fit into his social network. Catalysts think of who they know, who those people know, how they all relate to one another, and how they fit into a huge mental map. Catalysts don't just know more people; they also spend time thinking about how each person fits within their network.

Let's say that you want to raise money for your favorite charity—the local food bank. You might begin by thinking of the people you know, perhaps making a list, and then getting on the phone. You'd probably start by gently asking your good friends if they'd be willing to contribute. Maybe you'd venture to ask some coworkers or people from other areas of your life—your church or bowling team, for example.

Catalysts would go about the task in a completely different way. Like you, they'd begin by mapping out all the people they know who might contribute. But then they'd think about which people in their network could become advocates: "Alice owns a restaurant," they'd remember, "and all of her friends are passionate about food. Maybe I can get Alice to raise funds from forty of her friends. Or better yet, I can introduce her to Bill, a doctor who cares deeply about poverty, and the two of them can form a team to raise an endowment fund. Or better yet . . ." You get the idea.

Now, all of us map to a certain extent. But our maps tend to be small-scale and personal. If our personal maps are a sketch of a neighborhood or a city, the catalyst's map is a detailed satellite image of an entire country. Not only do catalysts navigate their maps with ease and speed, but they constantly pave new roads between towns—making new connections and forming new circles.

Desire to Help When we first started talking to catalysts, we were honestly surprised by how much each of them wanted to help. "Are these people for real?" we asked ourselves. Time and time again, the answer was a resounding, albeit surprising, "Yes, they are."

Wanting to help is the fuel that drives a catalyst's ability to connect people. If Josh Sage didn't want to help people, he wouldn't bother traveling around the country getting them engaged in social activism. Likewise, without the desire to help, Auren Hoffman would just enjoy meeting new people and forming acquaintance-type relationships. It's only because he wants to help that he actually connects people to one another.

What if a catalyst didn't care about helping others? He could make a few connections for purely personal gain, getting people in his network to do him favors. But if the network is one-way, that is, if it's all about helping the catalyst, then it would quickly get tapped out. People wouldn't return Auren's phone calls if they thought he was just trying to get something from them. They participate in his network because they benefit from being a member.

The desire to help people isn't just a nicety; it's an essential part of being a catalyst.

Passion Once Josh Sage puts his mind to something, chances are that it will get done; he locks on a target and doesn't waver. Josh has been working toward essentially the same goals for the past fifteen years. It's a relentless belief in his ideology, as well as boundless energy to pursue a goal, that drives Josh and makes him effective.

The catalyst provides the drumbeat for a decentralized organization. Because it can't draw upon command-and-control to motivate participants, it needs a strong and ongoing ideology to keep them going. The catalyst starts the organization and then takes on the role of constant cheerleader. But the catalyst must walk a fine line. If Josh cheered too much, the movement would become "The Josh Sage Show."

Meet People Where They Are There's a difference between being passionate and being pushy. A catalyst doesn't try to persuade people but rather relies on a much more subtle technique: meeting people where they are.

Let's say your friend tells you that he's unhappy with his job. Because you care about him, you listen and probably suggest some alternatives. Has he talked to his boss? Has he thought about a different career? Maybe he should take some time off.

If your friend's unhappiness lasts for a while, you might get more assertive in your suggestions: "You really need to talk to your boss," or, "I want you to interview for this new job." Noted psychologist Carl Rogers warned that this kind of expert advice-giving, though intended to help, actually has the opposite effect. When confronted with an aggressive push, most people shut down and become even less likely to change.

Rogers practiced a different approach. Rather than suggesting ways for his client to change, he would acknowledge their experience: "So, you're unhappy with your job. That must be difficult." The client might say, "Yeah, it's terrible. Every day I go in, and I immediately start counting the seconds till it's time to go home."

"It feels a little like being trapped, I imagine."

"Yes, exactly."

As Rogers focused on listening and acknowledging his client's experience, something amazing would happen. The client would find his own solution to the problem. "You know, I don't like being trapped. I think I'll look for a new job."

When people feel heard, when they feel understood and supported, they are more likely to change. A catalyst doesn't prescribe a solution, nor does he hit you over the head with one. Instead, he assumes a peer relationship and listens intently. You don't follow a catalyst because you have to—you follow a catalyst because he understands you.

When we give advice to someone, we automatically create a power hierarchy. The advice-giver is superior to the recipient. As we've seen, this kind of hierarchy is detrimental to a decentralized organization. In meeting people where they are, catalysts can inspire change without being coercive.

Emotional Intelligence If this is starting to sound like an episode of *Dr. Phil*, that's because a catalyst depends heavily on emotional intelligence. All the catalysts we've met are intellectually brilliant, but they tend to lead with emotions.

There's a good reason why Deborah refused to talk to the

advocacy groups about specific strategy. If she had talked nuts and bolts, it would have been much harder to form an emotional bond. To a catalyst, emotional connections come first. Once there's an emotional connection, then and only then is it time to brainstorm and talk strategy.

This type of emotional bond is present in most of the decentralized organizations we've seen. Craigslist users who have never met consider themselves part of the same community; AA members will go to great lengths just to help each other stay on the road to recovery.

The catalyst weaves emotional connections into the very fabric of the organization. People agreed to run projects for David Martin because they respected him and believed in him. The activists, likewise, called Deborah Alvarez-Rodriguez because they felt a personal kinship with and connection to her.

Trust It's not enough to meet people where they are and to form emotional bonds with them; a catalyst must also trust the network. With a flattened hierarchy, you never know what people are going to do. You can't control the outcomes, and you can't really reproach a member if he becomes errant. All you can control is whether people have personal relationships with each other based on trust.

Inspiration A true catalyst isn't just a matchmaker but also an inspiration to others to work toward a goal that often doesn't involve personal gain.

When you talk to Deborah, you think that Goodwill is the best organization in the world. When you speak with Josh, you want to forsake your car and ride a bicycle. When you talk to Jimmy Wales, you want to spend hours in front of the computer contributing to Wikipedia.

Think of the earliest contributors to Wikipedia, for example. At the time, the concept wasn't proven, and no one knew that the Web site would grow so dramatically. Yet people volunteered their time. It wasn't because they had stock options, it was because they believed in the big dream: that together people could build an encyclopedia that could be enjoyed by everyone around the world.

At the same time, none of the catalysts we met had a rock star quality to them. In fact, one catalyst sternly warned us, "Don't you dare make me out to be the hero. This isn't about me."

Tolerance for Ambiguity One of the most common answers we got when we talked to catalysts was "I don't know."

How many members does your organization have? "I don't know."

Who's in charge of your server software? "I don't know."

And so on.

Catalysts aren't absentminded. They often don't know because there aren't concrete answers to these questions. Being a catalyst requires a high tolerance for ambiguity. That's because a decentralized organization is so fluid that someone who needs order and structure would quickly go mad.

Think of Josh Sage in his RV, going from town to town starting circles. One day ten people show up at a meeting, the next day a hundred. One day people are excited, the next they're ambivalent. One circle excels, another falters. There's no way to measure results. There's no way to keep track of all the members. There's no way to even know who's doing what, let alone where and when. To an outsider, the chaos might appear overwhelming.

But this ambiguity creates a platform for creativity and innovation. Starfish organizations need ambiguity to survive. If someone came in and tried to implement order and structure, they might be able to get better measurements and tracking, but they'd kill the starfish in the process.

Hands-Off Approach Perhaps the most difficult and counterintuitive element of being a catalyst is getting out of the way. If Josh Sage kept looking over activists' shoulders, or if Jimmy Wales demanded daily reports from Wikipedia volunteers, the members of those networks would become unmotivated and the organization's creativity would come to a halt.

In a command-and-control environment, you can closely track what everyone is doing, but being watched and monitored makes employees less likely to take risks and innovate.

At the same time, when left to their own devices, members of a starfish organization can become frustrated with the catalyst. "What are we supposed to be doing?" they may ask. But it's precisely this question that leads people to take charge, giving members a high level of ownership over the organization.

Receding After catalysts map a network, make connections, build trust, and inspire people to act, what do they do? They leave.

If they were to stay around, catalysts might block the decentralized organization's growth. Deborah left her position with the City of San Francisco so that it wouldn't become all about her. Josh would leave town to allow the circles he'd formed to become cohesive units. Auren has to get out of the picture for the people he's introducing to be able to connect. He realizes that it's only in his absence that people take the reins and move their own relationships forward.

The Catalyst Versus the CEO

While both are leader types, catalysts and CEOs draw upon very different tools. A CEO is The Boss. He's in charge, and he occupies the top of the hierarchy. A catalyst interacts with people as a peer. He comes across as your friend. Because CEOs are at the top of the pyramid, they lead by command-and-control. Catalysts, on the other hand, depend on trust. CEOs must be rational; their job is to create shareholder value. Catalysts depend on emotional intelligence; their job is to create personal relationships. CEOs are powerful and directive; they're at the helm. Catalysts are inspirational and collaborative; they talk about ideology and urge people to work together to make the ideology a reality. Having power puts CEOs in the limelight. Catalysts avoid attention and tend to work behind the scenes. CEOs create order and structure; catalysts thrive on ambiguity and apparent chaos. A CEO's job is to maximize profit. A catalyst is usually mission-oriented.

But just because catalysts are different from CEOs doesn't mean that they don't have a place within organizations. Top-down hierarchy and structure can be repressive to the catalyst, but some

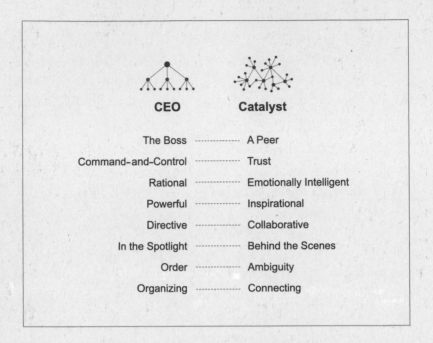

CEO	Catalyst
The Boss	A Peer
Command-and-Control	Trust
Rational	Emotionally Intelligent
Powerful	Inspirational
Directive	Collaborative
In the Spotlight	Behind the Scenes
Order	Ambiguity
Organizing	Connecting

situations are uniquely suited to catalysts. Want to figure out an innovative way to promote a new product, expand into a new market, build a community around your company, or improve employee relations? By all means, bring in a catalyst.

Take Deborah Alvarez-Rodriguez of Goodwill, for example. When she joined the company, morale was low, revenues were sluggish, and employee benefits were being cut left and right. The moment Deborah set foot inside, she began to enact massive changes. "I realized that I had to create a certain level of chaos," she told us. Her board, her management team, and the employees were scared. "Do you have to be so disruptive?" one board member asked. "Yes, I do," Deborah replied.

"We'd been such a hierarchical organization," she told us.

"We needed to get people into a conversation and get them to be innovative and creative. People in positions of power needed to understand that great ideas come from people who are closest to the ideas."

Deborah formed cross-functional brainstorming teams with about twelve members representing all levels of the company. Management had the final say, but it incorporated 95 percent of all suggestions made by the circles. Pretty soon Deborah's efforts paid off: the chaos she had created helped to decentralize the organization while at the same time seriously engaging employees. She increased both revenues and profits.

This type of leadership isn't ideal for all situations. Catalysts are bound to rock the boat. They are much better at being agents of change than guardians of tradition. Catalysts do well in situations that call for radical change and creative thinking. They bring innovation, but they're also likely to create a certain amount of chaos and ambiguity. Put them into a structured environment, and they might suffocate. But let them dream and they'll thrive.

CHAPTER 6

Taking On Decentralization

II.

The Long Haul Infoshop wasn't the kind of bookstore you see every day, even in Berkeley. On a November evening in 1995, fifteen people sat in the shop's back room. The group was eclectic: there were some students in their twenties, a couple of British guys, a few punk rockers, and a woman who looked like she'd be more comfortable at a Tupperware party than in this unlikely place. One by one, everyone introduced themselves. Despite their differing backgrounds, everyone in the group shared a common passion: animal rights.

It was time to get down to business, said Sky, who knew exactly what he was doing. At five-eleven, with neatly cut blond hair and a clean blue flannel shirt, Sky could have passed equally well as a college student, a lumberjack, or a wilderness guide. A few days earlier, Sky had arrived in Berkeley via rail. A freight train, to be exact. He had jumped on board at a yard in southern Oregon; between switching trains a few times and stopping over to visit some friends, the trip took him a little less than a week.

Now that everyone at the Long Haul meeting was focused on him, Sky spread out a topographical map on one of the beat-up tables and began teaching the group how to read it. He also taught them the essentials of compass navigation and how to use an air horn—all the tools necessary to sabotage a hunt. The idea was to go to public lands during hunting season and prevent wildlife from being shot. Wearing bright orange gear, the activists would follow the hunters until they spotted their prey. Then, just as the hunters prepared to shoot, the activists would blow an air horn and make a ruckus, scaring away the would-be prey.

The Tupperware woman began feeling anxious. "But the hunters," she said. "What if they try to shoot at *us?*" Sky wasn't fazed. "That's why you wear an orange jacket. They'd never shoot at you—it would be a homicide." The woman's fears weren't completely assuaged, and she looked uneasy as she mulled the implications of what Sky had just said. As for Sky, who never gave anyone his last name, he was used to these kinds of situations when he came into a new town. Some people fit naturally into the role of hunt saboteur; others didn't. But Sky never said anything negative or discouraging. His job, as he saw it, was to get a group on its feet. The members could eventually figure out who fit in, who didn't, and what actions to take together as a group.

In many ways, Sky was like a union organizer. He was also a

perfect example of a catalyst. He'd come into a progressive town like Berkeley and connect with the local animal rights activists. They usually weren't very difficult to find—every college town has at least one animal rights group, and the animal rights community is small and intimate enough that the major activists across different cities all know each other. For instance, Sky might be told, "When you're in Berkeley, look up Mike Jenkins, he knows what's up." Sky would pull into town, connect with Mike, and get to know him. If Mike seemed like a good, trustworthy individual, Sky would start asking questions like, "What do you think of direct action?" or, "Have you ever done a CD?" (A CD is an act of civil disobedience, like blockading the entrance to a building.) If Mike seemed receptive, Sky would ask him who else he knew who might be interested.

With Mike's help, Sky would pull together a group like the Long Haul saboteurs-in-training. This was all a part of a larger strategy. Sky would go from town to town and connect activists to one another. He'd then form a network that would allow them to collaborate—small circles all over the country working on various hunt sabotages. Because they'd be engaging in direct action for animals, this network of circles was, de facto, a part of the Animal Liberation Front (ALF), one of the biggest decentralized organizations in Europe and America.

The ALF was started in the early 1980s by a circle a lot like the Long Haul bunch. Activists began breaking into research labs to free the caged animals within; utilizing a modern version of the underground railroad, they would then find new homes for the animals. When other activists across the world heard of the break-ins, they got inspired and came up with their own acts of civil disobedience. Breaking into a lab had the excitement and appeal of a jewelry heist and the righteousness of a Robin Hood story.

At first, the labs didn't know what hit them, especially given that the general public, while not necessarily approving of the ALF's illegal activities, was shocked to learn about what happened behind closed doors at research facilities. After one break-in, for example, activists dressed in black ninja outfits released pictures of themselves cuddling rescued beagle dogs scarred from a burn study. In another case, the activists uncovered an internal video made by lab researchers in which a seemingly healthy primate was subjected to repeated head trauma. After the experiment, the researchers repeatedly poked fun at the now brain-damaged animal. These gory pictures and videos began to change public perception. After the images wore off, however, and after a few activists burned entire facilities to the ground, the labs went on the offensive. We can't have this kind of lawlessness, they argued.

The FBI got on the case, but like the Spanish attacking the Apaches, they met with little success. The ALF was just so different from what the FBI was used to dealing with. The FBI couldn't chop off the ALF's head because, as with the starfish, there wasn't a head to chop off. The ALF was a loose collection of circles, sparked by catalysts like Sky. They'd cooperate with one another on an informal basis, but circles were free to do whatever they wanted. Circles often got their inspiration and ideas from successful actions undertaken by other circles.

Ingrid Newkirk, founder of People for the Ethical Treatment of Animals (PETA), even published a mainstream book that read like an episode of *Mission: Impossible*. The book chronicles the actions of an ALF activist named "Valerie"—how she got involved, how she joined a circle, even how she broke into a lab. Newkirk's book lays out the ideology and provides a step-by-step guide to becoming an ALF activist. In the same vein, circles started publishing their own informal zines about how to carry out direct action (start a circle, befriend someone on the inside of a facility, scout the location, have a press plan, and so on).

From the very beginning, the FBI didn't have a snowball's chance. Agents did manage to infiltrate a few circles and even arrest and convict some activists. But those convicted just became heroes of the movement, inspiring even more activists to join the ALF. As for the labs, they realized that the ALF wasn't going away anytime soon. Just like AT&T and the record labels, they hunkered down. Labs became underground fortresses. If you visit the northwest corner of the UC Berkeley campus, for example, you'll find a large green lawn that looks like the perfect place for students to throw Frisbees on a sunny day. But if you look more closely, you'll see a host of security cameras and concrete stairs leading underground. The stairs lead to a massive, bunkerlike animal lab housing tens of thousands of animals. The Berkeley labs, which used to be spread out across campus, were too vulnerable to ALF attack. The university consolidated the labs into one structure, so as to better control access and improve security. Visitors are generally not allowed, and you can't just walk in off the street—not unless you can get through the security guards, the thick metal doors, and the bulletproof windows.

As we saw in the case of the Apaches and the P2P players, when attacked, decentralized organizations become even more decentralized. The opposite is true for spider organizations, and it's the eighth principle of decentralization: *when attacked, centralized organizations tend to become even more centralized.* They hunker down. The strategy works for research labs, but how about for a business? Or an entire country for that matter?

Although their ideologies are very different, the structural similarities between al Qaeda and the ALF are striking. The government's response to the 9/11 attacks, in turn, resembles the actions of the labs.

The ALF is fundamentally more an ideology than it is an organization. In a very real sense, *anyone* who takes action for animals is an animal liberator and is a part of the ALF. Likewise, al Qaeda is completely dependent on its ideology. Whereas the ALF was bolstered by the belief that animals should be treated respectfully, al Qaeda's ideology is strengthened by the fear that Westerners are threatening the fabric of Muslim civilization. That ideology is rooted in a perceived clash between Christian and Muslim cultures as old as the Crusades.

Just as Sky is able to channel activist ideology into direct action, catalysts like Osama bin Laden have been able to channel the rage over Western expansion and the invasion of Afghanistan into terrorist activities.

Likewise, al Qaeda circles have a lot in common with the Long Haul crew. Both depend on ordinary people who, when organized into circles and cells, gain immense power. Just as each lab break-in inspired other break-ins, al Qaeda's terrorist acts inspire others around the world to follow suit. Like AA before it, al Qaeda has begun to proliferate into countries like Spain, Saudi Arabia, England, and Jordan. Al Qaeda headquarters doesn't conceive each attack; rather, members adopt the ideology and copy what has worked in the past. Many unaffiliated groups simply take the brand and use it.

We saw this proliferation of circles firsthand when we visited

Kenya. Just outside of downtown Nairobi, the Kibera slum is the worst in Africa. Joseph, a warm man in his late fifties, was our guide as we walked unpaved streets where a million people live on six hundred crowded acres with no running water, no electricity, and no sewage service. The streets were muddy (at least we told ourselves it was mud), and there was garbage everywhere. The living conditions in Kibera are so harsh that the average life span is thirty-eight years—and dropping. A typical home in the slum is a nine-by-nine-foot tin shack where a family of eight to ten people is crowded together. What could be called the "living room" is typically separated from the "bedroom" by a torn bedsheet. We went inside several of these homes and for the first time in our lives fully realized what it's like to have absolutely nothing.

Although the people of Kibera don't have any of our material comforts, they are starting to see how we live—fancy cars, big houses, fast food. A part of them wants these comforts, but another part of them resents that Western expansion is changing their traditional way of life. In slums like Kibera, the resentment is so strong that at times people turn to extreme measures. If you're living in the slums, you can't start a traditional army, but you can start a circle. Imagine how stunned we were when Joseph, our guide, subtly gestured toward a group of middle-aged men sitting outside a doorway smoking and told us, "Look. Over there. See down that alley? There's an al Qaeda cell there."

Al Qaeda has reached the Kibera slum. Circles can communicate with one another through cell phones and e-mail; a cell in Kibera can now easily and regularly communicate with a cell in Kabul, Munich, or New York.

In response to al Qaeda's attacks, the U.S. government has

hunkered down and become more centralized. This is a big shift from its original roots as a fairly decentralized system. The Founding Fathers realized the importance of power distribution. The Constitution is therefore based on two key starfish principles. First, the government is divided into three branches, each of which is fairly autonomous and independent. Second, the Constitution purposely keeps the federal government weak, delegating significant power to the states.

Over the years, the federal government gradually became larger and more centralized. Centralization did have its advantages—the government established programs like a central banking system and currency, welfare to help the poor, the Environmental Protection Agency (EPA) to conserve resources, and Social Security for the elderly. The move toward centralization was gradual.

The events of September 11, 2001, however, greatly accelerated this process. It's a natural reaction, when attacked, to hunker down and adopt a command-and-control mentality. From this perspective, establishing the Department of Homeland Security makes perfect sense. But in a lot of ways, the move toward centralization is like yielding to Dave Garrison's French investors. After the 9/11 attacks, the United States sought out the leader of al Qaeda, much as the French investors sought the president of the Internet. The obvious target was Osama bin Laden, and the government put a $25 million bounty on his head.

There is a rationale for this strategy. Take a mythical mob family like the Sopranos. You have to assume that Tony is in charge because he is the smartest and most capable. If you take out Tony, the head, the family will scramble to find a replacement. Maybe Tony's cousin, who isn't as smart as Tony, will eventually take the helm. If you then kill Tony's cousin, his replacement will be even less capable, and so forth down the chain. The strategy makes perfect sense if you are fighting organized crime. But it falters when you take on a starfish organization. As we've learned from every starfish organization we've seen thus far, take away the catalyst and the starfish organization will do just fine. If anything, it'll be even stronger: if a catalyst is killed, the power shifts to the circles, making the organization that much more decentralized.

The U.S. government didn't just go after the catalyst, however. It also went after circles. But this tactic is no more effective than going after the catalyst. Take out a circle or two—or a hundred circles for that matter—and the decentralized organization does just fine. New circles sprout up like mushrooms. The government was repeating the same mistake the labs had made in combating the ALF. Not only that, but in an ironic twist, as the FBI pursued al Qaeda, it also relaunched its campaign against the ALF, labeling its members as domestic terrorists. The FBI conducted extensive surveillance, launched grand juries, and arrested activists. Some of these efforts may have had limited success, but the ALF is alive and well.

There are alternatives that can be more successful in the long term. We've seen how decentralized organizations are able to wreak havoc on a variety of industries and sectors, and we've also seen how the strategies used to combat these organizations fail. You'd think that the heads of corporations and governments would eventually retreat quietly and concede defeat to the decentralized opponent. But starfish are not invincible. Let's look at some concrete strategies to combat a starfish invasion. The first comes from the slums of Kenya, the second from the Southwest deserts, and the third from the Middle East.

STRATEGY 1: Changing Ideology

In the late 1990s, the Great Barrier Reef in Australia was suffering an explosion of starfish. There were so many starfish, in fact, that they were beginning to destroy the coral. A number of concerned divers decided to take matters into their own hands and formed a group called OUCH—the Order of Underwater Coral Heroes. They'd dive with their knives and cut the starfish in half to kill them.

The problem, of course, was that the halves generated entirely new starfish. OUCH was just making the problem worse. But one scientist had a solution. He understood that the two real culprits were water pollution and rising water temperatures. The only way to save the coral was to alleviate these environmental conditions. It might have been an uphill battle, but it was the only way to fight the starfish.

Similarly, given that eliminating the catalyst is a futile effort at best, and given that when you go after circles new ones quickly emerge, the only part of the decentralized organization that you *can* realistically go after is the ideology.

Take a look at what's happening in Kenya, for example. Amid the poverty in the slums of Kibera, we saw some inspiring glimmers of hope: a barbershop the size of a broom closet where a man proudly cut hair on a chair that looked older than he was; a makeshift outdoor grill where a woman sold fish and chips; kids hanging out around a tiny cinema with seven folding chairs and a TV–turned–movie screen.

Each of these small businesses—the barbershop, the grill, and the theater—were enabled by the Jamii Bora Trust. It all started when Ingrid Munro, a Swedish UN housing worker, decided to retire. The residents of the slums, who all knew and loved Munro, nicknamed her "the Volvo Lady," after the boxy old car she drove on the slum's muddy roads. Her other nickname was "Mama Ingrid." She was one of the only Westerners to go into the slums and truly embrace the residents—be they beggars, orphans, or criminals.

Mama Ingrid, a group of beggar women asked her, "What will we do without you if you retire? How will we live?" Munro knew that the only way there would be hope for these women was if they had the tools to lift themselves out of poverty. Munro told the group that if they started saving money, she would lend them twice as much as they had saved. So if a woman saved ten shillings, Munro would lend her twenty.

The women formed circles whose members guaranteed one another's loans. A bank for the poor in Kenya was born—and people no one had trusted before gained access to credit and a chance to create a better life for themselves. The circle of a few beggar women grew into an organization with more than 100,000 members—members like Janet, whose first loan was just enough to buy a potato to sell in the market. With the profits from the sale, she took out another loan so that she could buy two potatoes. The biggest day in her life, she said, was when she had enough money to buy a sack of potatoes. Now she was able to buy them wholesale. Potato by potato, she built a small business and was able to rise slowly out of poverty.

What a small loan can do is staggering. Beatrice Ngendo was a single grandmother who lived with her twelve grandchildren in Kibera. Her children and their spouses had all died of AIDS.

She said to herself: *I now have to work twice as hard as other mothers in Kibera to feed and educate these children.* Through her loans, Beatrice started four successful businesses: a grocery store, a butchery, a restaurant, and a stone boardinghouse that she built by hand. Her grandchildren gained access to education; when we met Beatrice, her oldest grandchild had just graduated as a qualified nurse.

Another Jamii Bora member was Wilson Maina, a charismatic figure with an infectious smile. Wilson was admired by many in Kibera: he ran a small business selling secondhand clothes. But just a few years earlier, Wilson had been a violent criminal. If not for the Jamii Bora loan, someone like Wilson would have been a prime candidate to join a terrorist cell. After all, he had nothing to lose. Things changed when he heard about Jamii Bora and realized to his astonishment that he was welcome to become a member. For the first time in his life, he found that people didn't look down on him but instead invited him to join. Wilson was stunned and moved that people could trust and believe in him. Having managed to change his own life, Wilson became active in counseling other young men to get out of crime.

With each loan that it gives, Jamii Bora is changing the ideology of the slums. The organization's effects aren't just humanitarian: Jamii Bora is one of the best weapons against al Qaeda. For years, the slums have been hopeless places where terrorists have easily recruited members—join us, they say, and we'll fight back. Jamii Bora changes the ideology from "Life is hopeless, so I might as well join a terrorist cell," to "There is hope—I can make my life better."

A continent away in Afghanistan, another remarkable organization is changing ideology one person and one community at a time. Future Generations asks a simple yet powerful question: how do you help communities use what they already have?

The organization doesn't send supplies to impoverished communities. Instead, it deploys catalysts. Take Abdullah, who was sent to the Bamian province of Afghanistan. This region is known for the Taliban's destruction of the giant Buddhas in 2001. Abdullah started the *poggel,* or "crazy," movement. He told people, "If you're so *poggel* as to believe a better world is possible, join the Poggel Party."

Membership in the party cost two hundred sun-dried bricks. With each person who joined, the *poggel* movement had more bricks. People started asking: what shall we do with all these bricks?

The answer was obvious—rebuild the community. Ex-combatants began collaborating and, in the process, learning about one another. With no outside money or support, the Poggel Party launched a network of 350 mosque-based literacy classes that are now teaching over 10,000 women and children. The organization is also involved in a community health worker program, reforestation projects, drought mitigation efforts, ditch irrigation, and even community-financed English and computer courses.

Like the members of Jamii Bora, Future Generations communities are lifting themselves up by the bootstraps. By improving living conditions in places like Kenya and Afghanistan, organizations are gradually changing the society's ideology. Similarly, what we call "Chinook diplomacy" is having a significant impact on perceptions of the United States in places like Pakistan and Kashmir.

A few weeks after the Kashmir earthquake of 2005, Rod visited the region. As soon as he left the airport in Islamabad, he heard a ground-shaking sound. Two huge Chinook helicopters were flying overhead. Rod was rattled, but then his driver turned around with a smile. Yelling over the noise, he said, "Look, they are great—these from America." No sooner had Rod checked into his hotel room than he heard the sound again. A pair of Chinooks was heading into the mountains, carrying desperately needed relief supplies into the area.

These Chinooks provided the most visceral experience of the relief operation. You heard the rotors from miles away and felt their vibration in your gut as the choppers approached. When they landed, you smelled the fuel and tasted the dust. This was what a relief effort looks, sounds, and smells like.

The United States couldn't have had better ambassadors. The Chinooks won the hearts and minds of tens of millions of Pakistanis and Kashmiris. Many people here had long-held anti-American sentiments, but when they saw these choppers bringing loads of urgently needed aid, the message was clear: Americans cared and were there to help.

The most striking image for Rod occurred when he was stuck in a traffic jam between Muzaffarabad and Islamabad. Coming up over the shoulder of the mountain, there were the Chinooks again. A small boy standing beside Rod's car window pointed up in the air, beaming, shouting to his father, and jumping up and down. His father, with a long beard and in traditional Kashmiri dress, said nothing. He just looked up and smiled. Despite the noise, there was a sense of calm in the air. These people's ideology was beginning to change.

But changing ideology isn't easy. As social psychologists know, it takes at least a month of concerted persuasion to change someone's ideology. Simply put, we don't change our worldviews overnight.

Ironically, Jamii Bora and the Chinooks are slowly succeeding in changing people's ideology because their mission isn't to change ideology but to help people. Because Jamii Bora genuinely wants to help, people respond in favorable ways. The process is very subtle and gradual. Try hitting people over the head, on the other hand, and you'll get a backlash. We become defensive and closed-off when we perceive that someone is trying to manipulate or control us.

That's exactly what happened when the Spanish tried to forcibly convert the Apaches to Christianity. To defend their ideology, the Apaches were willing to give up everything and fight Western culture for centuries. Some industries today are learning this lesson the hard way.

Take the movie industry's latest attempt to influence P2P downloaders, for example. The industry created public service announcements that are often added to the trailer section of DVDs. In pseudo-MTV style, one forty-five-second spot starts with quickly changing camera angles of a teenager at her computer downloading a movie. The rest goes something like this:

YOU WOULDN'T STEAL A CAR

flashes across the screen, followed by a scene of a kid stealing a parked car.

YOU WOULDN'T STEAL A HANDBAG

We see a guy in a suit lifting a woman's purse in an outdoor café.

YOU WOULDN'T STEAL A TELEVISION

A street thug lifts a TV from a back alley.

YOU WOULDN'T STEAL A MOVIE

We see a picture of a guy shoplifting a DVD.

DOWNLOADING PIRATED FILMS IS STEALING
STEALING IS AGAINST THE LAW

It's not surprising that the commercials quickly became a running joke among youth. The movie industry had tried to be cool and hip; they failed for the same reason that Nancy Reagan's "Just Say No" campaign fell flat on its face. The last things teenagers want to hear are messages from adults—trying to sound like teenagers—telling them that what they're doing isn't cool.

The current ideology among young people is "Why pay for music and movies when I can download them for free?" The movie industry is trying to change that ideology with clunky catchphrases like: "Don't support it, report it," and "Downloading pirated films is stealing."

When a starfish ideology can be successfully changed, the results are powerful, so theoretically, trying to change an ideology makes sense. But the process is difficult. Don't expect teenagers to be reciting the "don't support it, report it" mantra anytime soon.

STRATEGY 2: Centralize Them
(The Cow Approach)

When last we saw the Apaches, they were dominating the Southwest. The Spanish tried in vain to control them, and the Mexicans who followed had no better luck. When the Americans took control of the region, they too foundered. In fact, the Apaches remained a significant threat well into the twentieth century. But then the tide turned. The Americans prevailed. When Tom Nevins explained it to us, our jaws dropped to hear how something so simple could have such a big effect.

Nevins told us the story. "The thing is, the Apache were a threat up until 1914. The army still had a presence in the White Mountain reservation into the early part of the twentieth century." Why were the Apaches so difficult to defeat? Nant'ans emerged, Nevins said, and "people would support who they thought was the most effective leader based on his own actions or based on his behaviors. And it would happen fairly quickly." With new Nant'ans continuously emerging, the Americans finally "realized that they needed to attack the Apache at a very basic level in order to control them. It was a policy they first pioneered with the Navajo—who also were an Apache group—and they perfected with the Western Apache group."

Here's what broke Apache society: the Americans gave the

Nant'ans cattle. It was that simple. Once the Nant'ans had possession of a scarce resource—cows—their power shifted from symbolic to material. Where previously, the Nant'ans had led by example, now they could reward and punish tribe members by giving and withholding this resource.

The cows changed everything. Once the Nant'ans gained authoritative power, they began fighting each other for seats on newly created tribal councils and started behaving more and more like would-be "presidents of the Internet." Tribe members began lobbying the Nant'ans for more resources and became upset if the allocations didn't work out in their favor. The power structure, once flat, became hierarchical, with power concentrated at the top. This broke down Apache society. Nevins reflects, "The Apache have a central government now, but I think personally that it's a disaster for them because it creates a zero-sum battle over resources between lineages." With a more rigid power structure, the Apaches became similar to the Aztecs, and the Americans were able to control them.

Nearly a century later, in New York City, a similar pattern emerged at AA. Let's go back to when Bill W., AA's founder, made a crucial decision to relinquish control and allow the numerous circles to self-govern. Bill and AA members wrote down their life stories and the ways in which AA had worked for them. The idea was to keep the organization's ideology alive. Bill W. hoped that reading the book would be akin to hearing a speaker at an AA meeting.

As an ultimate act of letting go, Bill W. and his fellow authors agreed that all proceeds from the work, nicknamed *The Big Book*, would go to support Alcoholics Anonymous World Services, Inc., a nonprofit dedicated to supporting chapters world-wide. These proceeds weren't very significant when Bill W. put together *The Big Book*; AA had only about a hundred members at that time. He probably thought that revenues from the book would go toward buying chairs for meetings and printing fly-ers. But AA eventually grew into more than 100,000 chapters. Copies of *The Big Book* have sold like hotcakes over the years—22 million at last count. These unexpected book sales produced enormous revenues, all of which went to Alcoholics Anony-mous World Services, Inc.

What cows were to the Apache, book sales became to AA. As *Big Book* profits rolled in, the little nonprofit that they were sup-posed to fund ballooned into a huge, wealthy organization. What to do with all the extra money? Alcoholics Anonymous World Services, Inc., decided to spend a few million dollars to renovate its business offices. This got AA members grumbling. World Ser-vices executives had become self-proclaimed Montezumas. Most AA members, though, couldn't care less about headquarters. The value of the organization, after all, was in the circles.

When individual members of AA started translating *The Big Book* into various languages and giving it away for free, head-quarters cracked down, even going so far as to sue members. Like MGM, World Services went to court to protect its intellec-tual property. This act diminished the ability of chapters to self-govern and innovate. World Services was nudging AA toward centralization.

At the core of what happened with the Apaches and with AA was the concentration of power. Once people gain a right to property, be it cows or book royalties, they quickly seek out a centralized system to protect their interests. It's why we want our banks to be centralized. We want control, we want structure, we want reporting when it comes to our money.

The moment you introduce property rights into the equation, everything changes: the starfish organization turns into a spider. If you really want to centralize an organization, hand property rights to the catalyst and tell him to distribute resources as he sees fit. With power over property rights, the catalyst turns into a CEO and circles become competitive.

This is why Wikipedia faces danger if it raises too much money. Ironically, the system works because it's underfunded and because almost everyone is a volunteer. If coveted paid positions were introduced, turf battles and a hierarchical system might result. With concentrated power, Wikipedia would become more centralized and begin to lose its collaborative environment. Similarly, if Burning Man introduced VIP tickets that gave people access to better campsites and line-cutting privileges, participants would no longer be equals.

But what about organizations like eMule that are so decentralized that there isn't anybody to give property rights to? The labels *could* have stopped the avalanche had they created financial incentives for Napster, Kazaa, and eDonkey to keep things legal. But with the avalanche having gained so much momentum, the labels must turn to the third strategy.

STRATEGY 3: Decentralize Yourself
(If You Can't Beat 'Em . . . Join 'Em)

The two strategies we've seen thus far are aimed at changing or reducing the power and effectiveness of decentralized systems. Change the ideology, and you alter the basic DNA of the organization. Concentrate power and you create hierarchy—making the organization more centralized and easier to control.

The third strategy recognizes that decentralized organizations can be so resilient that it's hard to affect their internal structure. Thus, if you can't beat them, join them. The best opponent for a starfish organization is often another starfish.

Let's go back to the slums of Kenya and Joseph, our guide. How did Joseph know that the group in the house down the alley was an al Qaeda cell? Joseph wasn't a member himself, but he was a slum-dweller, and he knew what was going on in his neighborhood—who was friends with whom, which group of people was doing what where. Like Sheeran during the 1935 Florida Keys hurricane, Joseph had access to superior knowledge.

What if you could empower Joseph to take care of that al Qaeda cell in the Kenya slums? What if you gave him the resources and let him solve the problem by whatever means necessary? Joseph could start a circle to combat the al Qaeda circle, and the two would fight it out. This isn't just a theoretical approach. It's exactly what one Muslim country has been doing. For obvious safety reasons, we can't get into all the details of the story, but here's essentially what happened.

A few years ago, we met with a guy we'll call Mamoud, a

prominent businessman in a Muslim country. We spoke to him about al Qaeda and discussed our belief that it's a starfish organization. To illustrate the point, we asked him, "How many al Qaeda cells do you think there are?"

"I don't know," he said.

"What if you had to venture a guess?" we asked.

"I wish I could. My government has been trying to figure this out, and they really have no idea." He explained to us that it wasn't for lack of trying. His country's government had spent significant funds and put massive resources into studying and combating al Qaeda. Mamoud was feeling frustrated: all this money and effort had been for naught, he confided. His government was no closer to eliminating the terrorist threat. In fact, it was getting worse by the day.

Speaking with Mamoud was a mixed experience. On the one hand, it was fascinating to learn that our theory about al Qaeda seemed correct. But on the other hand, it was discouraging to hear that no one had any idea how to combat the organization. Yes, you could try to change the ideology of al Qaeda adherents, and hope that would make an impact in the long run. And maybe governments could find a way to centralize and manage the organization (though Western governments have been doing the opposite: going after terrorist leaders and launching chains of events that make such organizations even more decentralized). But these are long-term strategies.

Two years later, Mamoud had some unexpected news.

"You know when we talked about 'that terrorist group' and the starfish?"

"Yes," we said.

"Well, we found a solution."

Mamoud's government had created small circles to combat al Qaeda. By day, the circles' members are police officers or former military experts—people who are well trained in conducting raid operations. By night, the circle members go out and hunt al Qaeda cells. The government supplies them with ammunition and doesn't ask many questions. The members of each circle don't know how many other circles there are, nor who's a member. Terrorist cells, meanwhile, don't know what hit them.

Human rights groups may object that the government is funding an undercover killing spree. We won't get into the political or moral implications of creating such circles, but one thing is for sure. Mamoud explained that although the program costs one one-hundredth as much as all the other efforts, it works better than anything else his government has tried. Explained Mamoud, "We can barely believe it ourselves. It works. It works because these guys know what's going on in their communities. They know who's a terrorist. They know where they live. And"—he smiles—"they know how to get them."

The record labels have attempted what at first appears to be a variation on this strategy. The industry has spread empty and corrupted song and movie files onto the P2P networks. The reasoning is that if there's lots of garbage on the network, it will no longer be worthwhile to spend time downloading songs. Yet again, however, the labels' efforts have backfired. Users don't mind encountering the occasional corrupted file—it comes with the territory.

And the labels look that much more draconian for proliferating garbage, so why not swap files and stick it to them? A different strategy could be accepting that music distribution channels have changed forever. Or perhaps the record labels could do the unthinkable: give out the music for free and let the music-swappers share files until the cows come home. Revenues would come from auxiliary sources—live concerts, merchandising, and corporate sponsorship.

But the bigger picture is what's important. In the decentralized revolution, old strategies don't work. A company or corporation must explore new options in order to effectively fend off a starfish attack. As we'll see, sometimes it's best to draw upon both the centralized and decentralized worlds—what we call "the combo special."

CHAPTER 7

The Combo Special:

The Hybrid Organization

One of the best places in the world to find suits at bargain prices is eClass229. In preparation to meet publishers in New York, we decided to buy matching Ermenegildo Zegna suits. It might have been cheesy, but we wanted to come into the meetings looking like a unified team. We arrived at eClass229 sniffing out bargains—try as we might, we just couldn't bring ourselves to pay full price.

The online eClass229 store has a homemade feel to it, and its logo features a computer font straight out of the early 1980s. There are a few low-resolution reproductions of top designers' insignias, all in different sizes and squeezed together to the point of overlapping. Before the days of the Internet, we would have opted to go to a known tailor or to a large department store. We might have paid more for the suit, but we'd have been assured it was genuine and of good quality. The bargains offered by eClass229 would have seemed too good to be true—like buying a Rolex from a guy standing on a street corner in Times Square.

But eClass229 is nothing like the Rolex guy. There's brilliance and beauty in eClass229; to understand it, we need to go back again to 1995. In that year, David Garrison met with the French investors, craigslist was founded, Netscape went public, and the folks at a new company called Onsale were positioned to take the world by storm. Backed by top venture capitalists, Onsale was one of the first online auction houses. It had money and what seemed like a great business model: auctioning off refurbished computers to the Internet's early users. The problem with an online auction, of course, is that you're buying something sight unseen from a seller you don't know from Adam. If you're going to spend hundreds of dollars for a used laptop, you want to know the seller is trustworthy. That's why Onsale obtained its laptops from select vendors and stood behind its products.

Onsale attracted lots of customers who were happy to get bargains on computers, and its stock price shot through the roof. But then along came Pierre Omidyar, a computer programmer whose fiancée couldn't find anyplace to buy her favorite collectible, Pez dispensers. Like Shawn Fanning, the creator of Napster, Omidyar took matters into his own hands, never realizing the massive force he was about to unleash. The service, originally called "AuctionWeb" but soon renamed "eBay," at first glance appeared similar to Onsale. But eBay had what seemed like a radical idea at the time. It allowed users to sell items directly to each other. It never took control of inventory and never served as an intermediary. After all, there was really no need to have a money-back guarantee for Pez dispensers.

In true catalyst fashion, Omidyar created a network based on trust. From the get-go, eBay declared, "We believe people are basically good. We believe everyone has something to contribute. We believe that an honest and open environment can bring out the best in people." Because eBay opened the doors wide and allowed anyone to sell any item as long as it was legal, the site quickly became home to a huge number of listings—from Pez dispensers to laptop computers to rare antiques. Users began flocking to the site, and eBay became the market leader.

Trust wasn't just a promotional scheme eBay cooked up to make users feel better about the site. From the beginning, trust permeated the entire company. Even today, when eBay employees consider a strategic decision, they are *required* to begin with the assumption that people are basically good and trustworthy.

Trust is vital, Omidyar understood. To ensure that people could continue to trust one another, he added a simple but crucial element to the site, one that proved key to eBay's ability to stay alive: user ratings. Buyers and sellers could give each other positive, negative, or neutral feedback, which was made public on the site. In empowering the community, eBay shifted the burden of policing from the company to its users—knowledge and power became distributed throughout the network. People only wanted to buy from sellers with high positive ratings; sellers gained a huge incentive to stay honest and trustworthy. A positive or negative rating, according to Harvard researchers, has real-life consequences. Items sold by users with an established record of positive feedback fetched an 8.1 percent premium over identical items sold by nonestablished sellers.

That's where eClass229 comes in. Despite its look, the company's eBay store had more than five thousand positive reviews and no negative ones. With a record like that, we felt we could trust eClass229. Indeed, the suits arrived in perfect condition a week later. Just to make sure, we took them to a tailor, who confirmed they were genuine Zegnas, and we wore them to our meetings (though no one seemed to notice).

Reputation alone sustains eClass229. Instead of pouring money into expensive branding and marketing campaigns, the company focuses on delivering quality and reliability. Similarly, tens of thousands of brick-and-mortar shopkeepers have closed their doors in favor of launching successful online eBay stores.

But although eBay hosts user-to-user interactions and relies on a decentralized user rating system, the company itself is no starfish. Like MGM, it has a CEO, a headquarters, a hierarchy, and a well-defined structure. If you go to its San Jose headquarters, you won't find an amorphous network; you'll find a forty-eight-acre corporate campus housing two million square feet of office space.

Up to this point, we've looked at companies at one end of the centralization continuum or the other; eBay represents the combo special. It's neither a pure starfish nor a pure spider, but what we call a hybrid organization. Companies like eBay combine the best of both worlds—the bottom-up approach of decentralization and the structure, control, and resulting profit potential of centralization. Representing the first of two types of hybrid organizations, eBay is *a centralized company that decentralizes the customer experience.*

A hybrid approach led to eBay's success, but it also created tensions. People are willing to trust one another when it comes to user ratings, but in other situations they want the safeguards that are possible only with a command-and-control structure. Seeing thousands of positive reviews, we were willing to trust eClass229 to send us genuine Zegna suits. But we'd be foolish to give the store direct access to our personal bank accounts.

That's why eBay's acquisition of PayPal was a smart and necessary centralized move. PayPal allows users to transfer funds to one another via a trusted intermediary. The eBay subsidiary is based on rigid controls and secure interactions. When it comes to banking, the eMule model doesn't work. PayPal never gives out a user's bank account information; this is a case where safety, structure, and accountability are necessary.

But the PayPal acquisition also created a clash of cultures. Although eBay is based on trust, as one PayPal employee told us, "If you were to tell someone at PayPal that people are basically good, they'd laugh in your face. We've seen too many shenanigans." While promoting trust, eBay also ensures safety through PayPal. One PayPal ad said it all: "SHOP WITHOUT SHARING . . . ," it announced in huge letters, adding in smaller print, ". . . your financial information."

Still, eBay's competitive advantage is deeply rooted in its decentralization. Let's look at what happened when Yahoo and Amazon, two of the biggest powerhouses at the time, saw eBay's auctions and asked: why can't we do that too?

On the surface it didn't look like eBay had anything so complicated and unique that it couldn't be copied. It let people list their items, it had some software to track auction bids, and otherwise it basically left people on their own.

Indeed, Yahoo and Amazon developed their own auction sites

offering similar services. Not only that, but they also did away with listing fees. They figured that sellers, realizing they could improve their bottom lines by paying no fees, would migrate to the new services. But surprisingly, that didn't happen.

Yahoo's and Amazon's strategy might very well have succeeded had eBay been centralized. Choosing among services that are identical except that some are free and some cost money is a no-brainer. The reason why sellers stayed with eBay and why it prevailed lies with eClass229 and the results of the Harvard study.

In short, it's all about reputation. You don't buy a suit from eClass229 because of the store's elaborate marketing or snazzy look. You shop there because five thousand other people recommend the store to you. Buyers were reluctant to switch to a new auction site where sellers didn't have a proven track record; they preferred to stay at eBay. Likewise, sellers with established positive ratings on eBay had a huge incentive to stay on the site rather than go elsewhere and start anew. For one thing, they were able to fetch premium prices based on their established reputations. They also had an incentive to stay where the buyers were.

In addition, eBay benefited from what's called the "network effect." Say there's only one telephone in the world. It's not going to be worth much, right? After all, who are you going to call? But when there are two telephones, their value goes up dramatically. Each additional telephone adds value to the overall phone system.

Likewise, eBay's network becomes more valuable with each new user rating. One user rating doesn't do anyone much good. But millions of ratings on millions of users have immense value.

The more the network grows, the more useful it becomes, and the more likely it is that customers will stay put. When new technology comes along (say, Skype in the case of telephones), people may eventually switch. But so far, no one's been able to come up with a better technology than eBay's user rating system. Buyers and sellers therefore stay at eBay—it's where the action is, and it's where they can find a network of trusted buyers and sellers.

The decentralized user ratings proved to be eBay's biggest competitive advantage. Because of eBay's hybrid solution, competitors couldn't attract buyers.

As for Amazon, although it couldn't capture many of eBay's auctions, it was able to grab a part of the decentralized retail market of books, CDs, and DVDs. For such low-cost items, a lower listing price does make a difference. Side by side with its own listings, Amazon allows independent sellers to list their merchandise as well. Like eBay, Amazon is a hybrid organization. Like most centralized organizations, it has a CEO, a headquarters, and warehouses, but it also has an intriguing decentralized feature.

If you browse for virtually any book on Amazon, chances are you'll find both an expert's review of the book (say, *Publishers Weekly*) and user-generated reviews. These reviews are really quite remarkable. For instance, when we recently shopped for Jared Diamond's *Collapse: How Societies Choose to Fail or Succeed*, we instinctively scrolled past the experts' reviews and looked for what other users had to say. We gave a lot of credence to the anecdotal reviews, not because they were necessarily more accurate or better written than those of the experts, but because they seemed, well, friendlier and more accessible. Reading user reviews is like talking to your neighbors about your favorite books.

Take, for instance, the reviewer J. P. G. Cox, otherwise known as "jpgm." We didn't know who jpgm was: we didn't know jpgm's name, age, occupation, or even gender. Yet we put great stock in jpgm's opinion of Diamond's book (jpgm gave the book five out of five stars and found it to be a "necessary" read). His or her comments came across as authentic—it seemed clear that this person was giving an honest opinion with no agenda.

Amazon keeps track of how many people find a user's reviews to be useful; 295 out of 350 found jpgm's comments helpful. We deemed jpgm's opinion to be valid for the sole reason that most other people deemed it valid and important as well. In other words, we trusted jpgm because others did. Trust begets trust.

Meanwhile, jpgm has written more than twenty reviews for Amazon. Let's think about this from jpgm's perspective. This person is writing all these reviews for a large corporation that doesn't pay a penny in return. Amazon, in fact, holds the intellectual property rights for reviews and even has patents on the technology for submitting them. Also, unlike eBay, where users depend on feedback to keep the system going, contributions to Amazon are nice but not essential. So the reviewers' motivation is not to keep the system going so that its success will benefit them. In fact, people would seem to have no incentive at all to contribute reviews.

So why do users work so diligently to provide reviews? It's certainly not to help out Amazon's CEO. It's probably not to help authors, although many authors have recognized the power of Amazon's reviewers and regularly send them copies of new books. And it's not for the small fame involved in being a featured reviewer. The forces that motivate jpgm to write reviews are the very same ones that inspire people to edit Wikipedia articles: everyone wants to contribute, and everyone has something to contribute somewhere.

Meanwhile, Amazon is happily capitalizing on these acts of generosity. The company has tapped people's desire for community and channeled it into a decentralized network of reviewers.

It's this same desire for community that catapulted Jacquelyn Mitchard, a mother of three and a speechwriter at the University of Wisconsin at Madison, to fame. One night Jacquelyn had a dream about a woman whose son was kidnapped. In casual conversation, she told her friend about the dream. The friend, who was a novelist, was fascinated and encouraged Jacquelyn to turn the story of the dream into a book. *Who am I to write a book?* Jacquelyn wondered. But a part of her just had to tell the story. She based her book *The Deep End of the Ocean* on her dream.

Jacquelyn was surprised that she was able to sell the book, and *The Deep End of the Ocean* did okay in the market. That is, until Jacquelyn was approached by Oprah Winfrey, who was just launching her now-famous book club. Jacquelyn was told that her book would be the first—and, depending on whether the book club idea took root or not, possibly the last—book on the list.

The original idea behind Oprah's Book Club was to inspire members of her audience to read good novels and to take time for themselves. She encouraged her viewers to form small circles where they could share feelings, reflect, and discuss a good book together. Any title that Oprah recommended was bound to see a boost in sales; she is, after all, one of the most admired and influential figures in media history. But the astronomical sales of

Jacquelyn's book couldn't be explained by Oprah's recommendation alone. The book club circles quickly became a strong force that turned Oprah's boost into an avalanche. Members of Oprah's Book Club bought *The Deep End of the Ocean* in droves. Within just three weeks, Jacquelyn's work, which had been at best a marginal success, shot to the top of the *New York Times* bestseller list.

Over the next few years, as book clubs spread, Oprah recommended dozens of other titles. Inclusion in the club meant skyrocketing sales. Unintentionally, Oprah became one of the most influential figures in publishing. She never received a cut of book sales; instead, she catalyzed a network of readers and created a decentralized community with unexpected power. While Oprah's production company remained centralized, she had added a decentralized element to her show.

In all of these cases, organizations introduced decentralized elements by giving their customers a role: eBay turned over the policing of the site to its users; Amazon encouraged any reader—however educated or well read—to review book titles; and Oprah created circles where her viewers became a coveted customer bloc in the publishing industry.

Looking at the success of some of these hybrid companies, Scott Cook had an idea. Scott is the founder and head of Intuit, the maker of Quicken and Turbo Tax software. When Scott saw Wikipedia and started thinking about the Amazon reviews, he was struck by how much people want to contribute and help each other out. Scott noticed that his accountant customers were posting questions on discussion boards about how to perform various tasks in Quicken. These questions would get answered incredibly quickly and skillfully. In fact, some of the answers that users provided were so good that they warranted inclusion in the official tech support documents. Some even made it into the next release of the software.

To facilitate these kinds of decentralized user interactions, in 2005 Intuit launched TaxAlmanac.org, a Wikipedia equivalent for tax issues. "One of the things that we've learned," explains the site, "is that the community wants to interact with one another." Indeed, this new wiki already has over eight thousand articles on topics ranging from how to record "ministers' compensation & housing allowance" to tips on filling out IRS form 8508. The site looks strikingly similar to Wikipedia, and any user can edit an article.

Interestingly, Intuit doesn't brand the site—you have to work hard to find any indication on TaxAlmanac.org that it is run by Intuit. Also, there's no mention of any products, Intuit-made or otherwise. The site is about building community. A strong brand presence would deter users, who might think the site was part of a promotional campaign. "So, what's the catch?" Intuit preemptively asks. "There is no catch. Intuit believes that collectively the tax professional community is smarter than any one individual. The collective knowledge of the entire tax professional community is far more powerful than any handful of experts." Intuit adds, "We are pleased to be able to facilitate the group knowledge and insight of tax pros from all walks of life. We are supporting this site as a way of giving back to the accounting community that has actively supported us."

While Intuit allows its users to help one another, Google, IBM, and Sun Microsystems have taken things a step further, inviting customers to actually make the product themselves.

Google's architecture is fundamentally based on user input. Its search algorithm works by scanning billions of Web pages to retrieve sites that other people have found useful. "Useful" is defined by how many other Web pages point to a page, how much traffic the page receives, and how many users click on the page link when it shows up in a Google search. In essence, doing a Google search is like running a popularity contest: which site on a given topic is most popular?

Google doesn't stop there. Its news site, for example, doesn't have a single editor who decides which news stories are important. Instead, the site displays links to the articles that are visited most often. In essence, when you go to Google News, you find what other people have found most relevant. Every time you click on a story, you in turn increase its importance. Because it depends on community input, the more people use Google, the more accurate it gets.

For some companies, decentralizing isn't just a matter of trying to succeed; it's a matter of survival. As in the music industry, starfish are wreaking havoc in the software industry. Unlike the litigious record labels, however, Sun and IBM have found innovative ways to ride the decentralized wave. IBM saw that Linux—the open-source operating system that rivals Microsoft Windows—was gaining traction. Instead of competing with the decentralized market entrants, IBM supported them. It deployed six hundred engineers whose sole job was to contribute to Linux, and it actively supported the development of Apache and Firefox, the open-source browser that competes with Microsoft's Internet Explorer.

IBM's strategy was based in part on the "whoever is my enemy's enemy is my friend" philosophy. That is, "if these programs are hurting Microsoft, our competitor, then let's help them." But it's not just about thwarting competitors. IBM has predicted that open-source is going to win out in the end. The company could spend resources developing competitive products, but chances are they ultimately would lose out. The open-source movement simply has too much momentum.

Rather than try to develop a competitive operating system in-house, IBM supported the development of Linux, then designed and sold hardware and software that was Linux-compatible. IBM is harnessing the collective skill of thousands of engineers working collaboratively worldwide, and at no cost to IBM.

All of a sudden, there's a new culture of collaboration among the world's leading technology companies. What would inspire Scott McNealy, the chairman of Sun, to tell us with pride, "We're building communities, we're sharing"? McNealy is no softy, and Sun is accountable to its shareholders. And yet the company has made its once-proprietary server software, which accounted for $100 million in sales each year, open-source.

McNealy may have philanthropic values, but the decision to give away the software also came from economic necessity. The entire industry has shifted. Once one company offers decentralized open-source software, its competitors must follow suit in order to stay in the game. As with the record labels and eMule, the moment one decentralized force came into play, the rest of the industry quickly began to shift.

Like IBM, Sun has opted to forgo revenues from software sales in favor of making money on auxiliary services and hardware. The price of software is rapidly declining to zero, and the big players are looking for other ways of making money.

As the software industry becomes more decentralized, an entirely new logic system is being adopted. To a casual observer, what's going on seems like something from *Alice in Wonderland*.

Who would ever have imagined, for example, that companies would race to give away their software for free?

But it gets weirder. McNealy explained that IBM and Sun have both come out with similar software offerings based on the same open-source platform. "If either one of us doesn't do a good job, you can switch," he said.

Wait a second. Let's take a step back. McNealy is touting customers' ability to switch away from Sun? Don't companies *want* their customers to be "stuck" using their product? That used to be the case, but the open-source movement has thrown the industry into chaos. The availability of free open-source alternatives means that customers have a lot more freedom to leave.

Because Sun can't lock its customers in, it has to take a Buddhist approach—a variation on the refrigerator-magnet proverb: "If you love someone, set them free. If they come back, they're yours; if they don't, they never were." "Over the last few years," McNealy told us, "we've let our customers leave Sun easily if we don't have price performance. Now I argue they're going to come back in droves remembering that we didn't hold them up."

Is this the wave of the future? As industries decentralize, will companies give their customers freedoms that were previously unimaginable? One thing's for sure: IBM's and Sun's hybrid solutions are the only way for them to remain competitive in an increasingly decentralizing industry. The combo special isn't just a nice option—it's often necessary for survival.

Google, Sun, and IBM have put their customers to work, while Intuit, Oprah, and Amazon have given them a voice. But there are other ways for centralized companies to capitalize on decentralization. This brings us to the second type of hybrid organization: *a centralized company that decentralizes internal parts of the business.* These companies have a CEO and some hierarchy, but they also have starfishlike DNA.

This distinction can be easy to miss; you may have to look deep inside the company to uncover these differences. General Electric, for example, appears to be as far removed from decentralization as a librarian is from a NASCAR driver. At first glance, GE is everything that eMule is not.

When Jack Welch, GE's charismatic leader, took the reins, GE was a highly centralized bureaucracy in need of a healthy overhaul. Although much has been written about Welch's values, his real genius was in decentralizing the massive organization. He separated GE into different units that had to perform as stand-alone businesses. Each unit maintained its own profit-and-loss statement. Units were so independent that if unit A wanted to buy a product from unit B, it had to pay the full market price. At first, this approach seemed ridiculous. Why would you intentionally segment your company? Why would you create distance between departments? Why would you eliminate the very advantage that being a large company affords?

But Welch's approach benefited GE because it made each unit accountable and did away with inefficiencies. The business rules across the company were: be number one or two in a market or get out, and generate high returns on investments. If a business unit failed in either of these areas, it was sold. Welch's method ensured that each unit was being run profitably, while allowing unit heads significant flexibility and independence. The plan worked. GE's market value skyrocketed. Valued at $12 billion in 1981, it was valued at $375 billion twenty-five years later.

Decentralization can indeed produce higher financial returns.

Just ask Tim Draper, a Silicon Valley venture capitalist who runs Draper Fisher Jurvetson (DFJ), one of the world's most successful venture capital firms. Draper's involvement with Hotmail made him keenly aware of the possibilities of networks.

The traditional venture capital model is a lot like a castle. The members of the court convene in one place, and gaining access to them is nearly impossible unless you know the right people. In fact, many venture capital firms won't even look at an entrepreneur's business plan unless it is referred by a trusted source. This model makes sense when you think about the volume of demands for capital: venture capitalists might miss a few deals here and there, but they have to impose filters or they'd be overwhelmed with proposals.

Draper turned this model upside down. Rather than centralizing in one or two offices, DFJ has nineteen U.S. offices and twenty-three abroad, with seventy-one partners—a number unheard of for most venture capital firms. The idea is to cast a wide net and leverage each partner's individual network in a given region. After all, a partner in Ukraine has much better knowledge and information about the region than someone sitting thousands of miles away in Silicon Valley. The breadth of the network also exposes DFJ to a wider variety of industries. "We would never have seen the deals we saw in nanotech without the network," Draper explained.

Unlocking the closed gates of the traditional venture capital firm, DFJ reviews each and every business plan that comes in. As Draper told us, "We will look at anything." What has the firm seen? Its keen understanding of networks led DFJ to invest in Skype. The firm owned 10 percent of the company when it was sold to eBay for $4.1 billion.

The decentralized genie has been let out of the bottle. As we've seen, it's futile to try to put the cap back on or to fight the genie using antiquated weapons. But that doesn't mean companies should surrender. A hybrid approach allows companies to gain from both worlds.

To benefit from decentralization, a company need not radically change its structure. Take, for example, David Cooperrider, a friendly and likable professor at Case Western Business School. In an academic environment that focuses on theory and quantitative research, Cooperrider is a practitioner who jokes that the only figures you'll find in his studies are the page numbers.

Cooperrider developed a process he calls "appreciative inquiry." When we first heard about the concept, it seemed too touchy-feely to be effective. But as we spent time with Cooperrider, and, more important, when we learned about the companies that had used his method, we truly began to appreciate his work.

On the surface, appreciative inquiry is, as the name suggests, based on people asking each other meaningful questions. Sounds simple enough, but when you view the process with a knowing eye, you realize it's a way of decentralizing an organization.

Here's how the process works. Cooperrider brings in people from all levels of the company, from the janitor to the CEO. He pairs up the participants, and each person interviews his or her partner. Cooperrider provides the questions, which are designed to encourage people to open up to each other and, in the process, break down hierarchical differences. People begin to see each other as individuals instead of as a boss or a subordinate.

After interviewing each other, participants form circles where they are encouraged to dream and brainstorm. They may talk, for example, about their vision for the organization, however seemingly "out there." During the brainstorming exercise, every idea—regardless of who came up with it—is given credence. Appreciative inquiry draws upon knowledge from the edge of the network. Low-level employees may have good data and creative ideas; without a process like appreciative inquiry, however, they would never have the chance to share those ideas face to face with the CEO. Because everyone feels they have been heard, participants become more likely to support a new plan. What might otherwise have been a top-down order from management now becomes an initiative that everyone is behind.

Critics might argue that appreciative inquiry is appropriate only for touchy-feely companies where employees are urged to *feel* and *share*. But appreciative inquiry has helped to resolve strife between management and unions in one of the biggest long-haul trucking companies in the world and to create a strategic plan in the U.S. Navy. When you can get truckers to talk about their personal dreams and aspirations and their vision for the company, you know you've hit upon something big.

In whatever form, the introduction of decentralized elements has helped companies ranging from eBay to IBM stay competitive. But the combo special requires a constant balancing act. As we'll soon find out, companies can't rest on their decentralized laurels; they must seek and pursue the elusive "sweet spot."

CHAPTER 8

In Search of the Sweet Spot

In 1943 future management legend Peter Drucker received a special invitation from General Motors to solve a mystery. At the time, GM was one of America's biggest and most respected companies; Drucker was determined to discover the secret behind its success. Little did he know that his investigation would unlock powers that were to influence industry for generations to come.

Drucker set about his task at GM much the way his grandmother would have. "She spoke to everybody the same way," Drucker later recalled in his autobiography, "in the same pleasant friendly voice, and with the same old-fashioned courtesy."

Drucker's grandmother was a big influence on him; she was the kind of person who wasn't afraid to rock the boat, but always did so with gentleness and kindness. The same could be said of Drucker, who was pleasant and thorough, but at the same time unafraid to ask deep and probing questions.

Drucker's inquisitiveness made his approach to understanding companies unique. Most researchers studying corporations focused their attention outside the firm. They'd look, for example, at what kind of marketing campaigns worked or what types of salesmen yielded the best results. In doing so, they missed a big part of the story: what happened inside the company to make it succeed or fail. This was the question that fascinated Drucker. He studied management in order to understand what really made businesses tick. The idea of analyzing management was completely foreign to many of Drucker's contemporaries. They assumed that management was a no-brainer: managers tell people what to do, and they do it. Where others saw a given, Drucker saw an intricate web of human interactions. How, he wondered, did power structure, political environment, information flow, decisionmaking, and managerial autonomy contribute to a company's success?

For Drucker, the GM assignment was a gold mine. Granted unrestricted access to the inner workings of one of the leading companies of the day, Drucker spent eighteen months gaining a rare in-depth understanding of the business. He was thorough, he was patient, and he was just as interested in people as he was in data. By the time he was finished, he had studied virtually every aspect of the business and understood GM as well as, if not better than, most of its top management. Most important, Drucker had developed a robust theory to explain GM's success.

Drucker was very well liked within the company. His questions were those of an astute observer who was truly intrigued by the company and had a genuine desire to learn more about it. So taken with him was GM that, unbeknownst to him at the time, the company seriously considered offering Drucker a top-level executive management job.

It seemed like a marriage made in heaven. That is, until Drucker came out with the results of his study. When his landmark work, *Concept of the Corporation*, was published, GM was furious. The company's top management viewed Drucker's book as a complete and utter betrayal. What was Drucker's betrayal of GM? In his book, he suggested that the company alter its strategy so as to benefit from becoming even more decentralized.

Drucker never intended to offend GM and was surprised by its reaction. In his mind, GM was a great company. In his study, Drucker even compared GM to the U.S. government, using the term "federal decentralization" to describe it. "In Federal Decentralization," he said, "a company is organized in a number of autonomous businesses." Just as the U.S. government ceded power to the states, GM gave autonomy to its divisions.

But GM's divisions weren't exactly the arms of a starfish; GM was more of a hybrid organization. The company had headquarters, a hierarchical structure, and centralized control. Unlike a purely spiderlike organization, however, GM delegated a high degree of power to its division managers. Each manager was empowered to make critical decisions while the executive team took on more of a catalyst role. The executive team primarily made suggestions about strategy and gently coaxed the division leaders. At GM, Drucker explained, "it is the right as well as the duty of every managerial employee to criticize a central management decision which he considers mistaken or ill-advised . . . such criticism is not only not penalized; it is encouraged as a sign of initiative and of an active interest in the business. It is always taken seriously and given real consideration."

Yes, the executive team had veto power over all decisions and ultimately had the final say, but these powers were rarely invoked. In addition to giving division managers autonomy, GM also ensured that each of them became independently wealthy. As a result, GM division managers came to work not out of dependence on a paycheck but to pursue a passion. This passion was the core of GM's ideology: we are here to excel.

Drucker argued that this decentralization was key to the success of GM. It freed top management to focus on larger issues, he explained; GM utilized decentralization as a way of efficiently distributing power around the organization. So why did GM get upset with Drucker? Because along with his praise he suggested that GM continue innovating and adopt more starfish concepts—for example, by asking customers what worked for them and what didn't and incorporating that feedback into corporate strategy (basically, empowering the customer, much as Sun, IBM, and Intuit would do decades later).

But GM's response was: Why should we change? We have something that works. Look, we're at the top of our industry—how dare you come in and make suggestions?

Compare GM's reaction with what happened when Drucker went to Japan, where his theories were listened to intently. Drucker later recalled, "I taught them that communication is to be upward if it is to work at all. . . . I taught them that top management is a function and a responsibility rather than a rank and a privilege." In other words, he taught the Japanese to embrace the hybrid organization.

Over the years, the Japanese continued to innovate, while companies like GM stuck with more traditional command-and-control management. The decision to remain stationary would end up costing GM. Let's fast-forward several decades and visit the assembly lines of GM and its Japanese competitor, Toyota.

A typical GM factory in the 1980s evoked every stereotype we have of an assembly line. Each worker was responsible for a single task, and the hierarchy was rigid and clear. If an employee made a mistake or detected a problem, he could stop the line, whereupon a loud alarm would sound. Workers would rush to solve the specific problem and get the line going again. But as many drivers could attest, the cars GM produced in the early 1980s were prone to mechanical failure. The system was producing cars that were at best okay, but definitely not great.

The Toyota assembly line was drastically different. Employees were regarded as members of a team, and each team member was considered an important contributor and given a high level of autonomy. What happened if an employee stopped the line? A pleasant "ding-dong" would sound and teams would carefully study what was going on, in an effort to continually improve the process. Line workers were constantly encouraged to make suggestions.

Take a moment and imagine that you're the head of Toyota. How many worker suggestions would you implement? Assuming that the majority of suggestions are well meaning but erroneous—15 percent? Playing the odds that half of the suggestions are likely to be helpful—50 percent? Try 100 percent. Just like Wikipedia edits, each and every suggestion made by a Toyota line worker was implemented. In decentralized fashion, teams functioned like a circle, and whatever ideas employees had for innovation were put into practice. And in Wikipedia fashion, if someone's suggestion proved counterproductive, another employee would inevitably make a suggestion to undo the previous suggestion.

This was an entirely different way of dealing with employees. Rather than regarding line workers as drones who had to follow directions and be kept in line, Toyota viewed its employees as key assets. Imagine the line workers' feeling of empowerment. Their opinions mattered. But Toyota didn't stop there. It also flattened its management hierarchy and equalized the pay scale. Now everyone was in it together. The net result of these innovations was that the cars Toyota produced were of dramatically higher quality than the vehicles that left a GM plant.

Experts tried to explain why Toyota plants were able to produce a high-quality product and foster efficient teamwork while GM's were not. Some speculated that GM's problems arose from the growing power of unions. Others, including Drucker, attributed the Japanese success to cultural differences. The Japanese, he said, had "come to accept my position that the end of business is not 'to make money.' " Drucker then got philosophical: "The Confucian concept, which the West shares, assumes that the purpose of learning is to qualify oneself for a new, different, and bigger job . . . within a certain period of time the student reaches a plateau of proficiency, where he then stays forever. The Japanese concept may be called the 'Zen approach.' The purpose of learning is self-improvement. It qualifies a man to do his present task with continually wider vision, continually increasing competence, and continually rising demands on himself."

"Culture-schmulture," the Japanese retorted. The differences had nothing to do with unions, cultures, or Confucian and Zen philosophy. To prove its point, Toyota asserted that, with its help, GM could achieve the same levels of quality.

GM was intrigued. To see if Toyota was just blowing smoke, GM proposed that the Japanese take over management of its Fremont, California, auto plant, one of the company's lowest-producing plants. The quality of the vehicles that rolled out of the plant was awful, the union had a terrible relationship with management—who even carried guns for protection—and daily absenteeism was at a staggering 20 percent. The plant was so bad, in fact, that GM had decided to close it down.

GM's challenge to the Japanese was: here you go, let's see what you can do with the Fremont plant—but, oh, by the way, you have to hire the same union force. No problem, replied Toyota. The two companies reopened the Fremont plant, renaming it New United Motors Manufacturing, Inc. (NUMMI).

Toyota management implemented the same procedures that had worked so well in Japan and brought hybrid organization principles to Fremont. "Our team dictates what we do and how we do it. Our group leader comes by about a half-hour per week," recalled one employee. "I feel that the team members are what's most important. We can function without management."

. The results were staggering. Within three years, the new plant had become one of GM's most efficient. NUMMI's productivity, in fact, was 60 percent higher than at comparable GM plants. Along with productivity, quality dramatically improved.

The story of Jamie Hresko, a production manager at GM's Buick City plant, says it all. Hresko decided to conduct an experiment. There was a way, he figured, to muck up the NUMMI process; after all, they couldn't be *that* perfect.

Hresko managed to get hired as a line worker at NUMMI. Don't give me special treatment, he told the managers, and don't tell anyone I'm a manager at a different plant. Once hired, Hresko conducted a one-man sabotage campaign. For a month, he slacked off and broke the rules, doing things like coming in late from lunch or creating a safety hazard by stacking parts on the floor. In each case, he wasn't reprimanded by management; instead, his team members admonished him. Hresko could hardly believe it. The union workers, once the thorn in GM's side, now wanted to make sure that the plant was running smoothly. This was hardly the same plant that GM had decided to close down a few years earlier.

Now, if parts of this story sound familiar, it's because the NUMMI plant was the inspiration for the movie *Gung Ho*. Except that the movie doesn't quite capture the real reason for the plant's success. It suggests that the improvement came about through rigid Japanese control. In the film, the American workers learn to stop slacking off, the Japanese learn to take it easy once in a while, and everyone lives happily ever after.

But NUMMI's success wasn't about rigid management. Nor was it about cultural differences or union politics. While good management and alignment of incentives did have something to do with it, the success really stemmed from Toyota's continual pursuit of the decentralized "sweet spot."

Let's revisit GM's reaction in the 1940s when Drucker came out with his book. Basically, GM was unwilling to change. It was a hybrid organization, but it refused to explore strategies for becoming more decentralized. Why mess with a good thing? reasoned GM's management. Toyota, on the other hand, continually strove to find the ideal balance between starfish and spider systems.

The decentralized sweet spot is the point along the centralized-decentralized continuum that yields the best competitive position. In a way, finding the sweet spot is like Goldilocks eating the various bowls of porridge: this one is too hot, this one is too cold, but this one is just right.

Let's take another look at the online auction industry. As we saw, around the same time that eBay was founded, another auction house entered the market. Onsale was funded by some of the top venture capitalist firms in the Silicon Valley and was the darling of the investment community.

Onsale began by selling new and refurbished computers. The company would either buy computers directly from the manufacturer and resell them or act as an intermediary, allowing vendors to sell directly to consumers and charging a commission. At the time, Onsale's business model made a lot of sense. There was a supply of computers that typically sold for dramatically reduced prices, and there was a demand from customers who wanted to get a good deal on electronics.

There were challenges in managing inventory and quality control, but they were manageable. Onsale held and sold inventory like other vendors, but rather than charging a set price, it allowed consumers to bid against one another. Onsale managed the inventory and offered between 500 and 1,200 items on any given day. It was a centralized solution that took a small step toward decentralization: bidders were encouraged to form a community by posting playful taunts as they bid against one another. The Onsale concept worked fairly well and had good potential. Indeed, as it gained popularity, Onsale became the biggest and most successful online auction house, and its stock price sky-rocketed.

But when people started using eBay, the market dramatically shifted. Compared to Onsale's small step, eBay took a giant leap toward decentralization by allowing anyone to sell and purchase items. Why would users select from a list of a few hundred items offered by a handful of vendors when they could select among thousands of items offered by thousands of people on eBay?

Onsale began losing market share and soon went out of business. The decentralized system that allowed eBay users to auction items directly to each other was simply superior—eBay had landed on the sweet spot. Compared with eBay, craigslist was too decentralized: because it allowed anyone to post and didn't offer user ratings, the site wasn't conducive to the sale and purchase of expensive items, at least not sight unseen. But eBay has managed to strike the balance between the spider and starfish organizations. Unlike Onsale, it doesn't house inventory from vendors. Unlike craigslist, however, it doesn't depend on trust alone. User ratings on eBay create a combination of trust and security.

If eBay were to become more decentralized, it would lose customers. For example, if eBay didn't verify users' e-mail addresses and allowed anybody and everybody to post anonymously, there wouldn't be as much accountability. Less accountability would translate into diminished trust, and users would become more wary of buying items sight unseen. Likewise, if eBay were to become more centralized—say, by verifying the quality of the goods sold—commissions would become higher, and it would no longer be economical to sell on eBay. Again, this would drive away customers and reduce revenues. The company would lose market share if it moved further toward either centralization or decentralization.

Toyota occupied the decentralized sweet spot in the automotive industry. Had it centralized its assembly line to mirror GM's, it would have taken power away from employees and reduced vehicle quality. But on the other hand, had Toyota decentralized too far—doing away with structure and controls and, say, letting each circle work on whatever car it felt like—the company would have had a mess on its hands. Decentralization brings out creativity, but it also creates variance. One Toyota circle might very well make a wonderful automobile, while another might produce a junker.

The sweet spot that Toyota found has enough decentralization for creativity, but sufficient structure and controls to ensure consistency.

It seems that Drucker intuitively understood the concept of the decentralized sweet spot. Just because you're on the sweet spot now (as General Motors was in the 1940s) doesn't mean it won't shift in the future. In some cases, like the online auction industry, the sweet spot seems to be fairly stable. In other cases, however, it is much more mercurial and must continually be pursued.

Let's take another look at the music industry. For centuries, the industry was decentralized, being nothing more than the performances of individual musicians. When the phonograph was invented, all of a sudden people could make a lot more money by running a record label than by being an individual artist. The sweet spot had shifted toward the centralized end of the spectrum.

As more record labels came onto the scene, there was even more money to be made by consolidating them into mega-labels. Economies of scale came into play: the larger the asset base and distribution network, the lower the cost per asset. (Economies of scale work in favor of Wal-Mart, for example, because it's more efficient to run a host of large stores that sell everything than it is for small, independently owned stores to sell a narrow class of goods.) For instance, a number of small record labels must each carry the costs of maintaining a recording studio and supporting talent scouts, producers, a legal team to draft contracts, and a marketing department to promote titles. But if the many small labels are aggregated into a single powerhouse, like Sony, redundancies can be eliminated because the company needs only one legal team, one marketing department, and so on.

Now, all was well and good for the record labels until Napster came along and made peer-to-peer music-sharing possible, dramatically shifting the sweet spot toward decentralization. In this new scenario, eMule was certainly too decentralized to be a profitable model—it produced no revenues, let alone profits. But the music labels were too centralized: they were losing money. This shift, however, also created opportunity. Just ask Apple, maker of the ubiquitous iPod. Apple realized that music listeners were getting increasingly frustrated with hearing a song on the radio and going out and purchasing it on CD, only to find out that the rest of the album was garbage. Although many were happy to illegally download songs for free, others were hesitant to pirate music and were willing instead to pay for a specific song, just not the whole album. That's where Apple's online music store, iTunes, came in: iTunes began selling individual songs for ninety-nine cents each, and it was all perfectly legal. Apple understood that the record labels were too centralized, but that the illegal offerings of services like eMule posed too big a risk for many consumers.

Apple also realized that users wanted to share content with one another. It therefore encouraged users to "podcast," or broadcast their own programming to other users—anything from a cooking show to a question-and-answer session with Senator John Edwards. Apple has proven that when centralized and decentralized forces take each other on—in this case, the record labels and the music-swapping services—there's money to be made from adopting the middle-ground approach.

Apple may be sitting pretty on the sweet spot today, but that's no guarantee that the sweet spot won't shift tomorrow. It's almost like a tug-of-war: the forces of centralization and decentralization continue to pull the sweet spot to and fro. But understanding that the sweet spot can move and predicting these tectonic shifts are two very different things.

In the music industry, for example, could the labels have predicted that the sweet spot was about to shift so suddenly and dramatically? The answer turns out to be a surprising yes—if only they had asked the right questions. The record labels had long known that people like to copy music. More broadly, we have a natural human tendency to share information. That's why keeping government and corporate secrets is so difficult—people are apt to gab. Once the peer-to-peer technology was out there, the writing was on the wall.

People's propensity to share music is precisely why the labels have fought for antipiracy laws and tried to block new technologies, like the CD burner, that make copying music easier. For a while, these measures sorta kinda worked. Yeah, people burned CDs for friends, but the amount of piracy was fairly contained. Anyone who tried to sell massive numbers of bootleg copies in the United States faced stiff penalties.

The Internet made sharing songs a cinch. But still, anyone who openly enabled music-swapping—like Napster, for example—was exposed to lawsuits. People's only option was to become more anonymous, using services like eMule. Up against the wall, people turned to decentralized options. Starfish organizations are wonderful places for those who want to freely share information, and better yet, they can easily serve as hosts to anonymous sharing. Together, these two forces, anonymity and free information flow, made the industry more decentralized and shifted the sweet spot.

In any industry that's based on information—whether it's music, software, or telephones—these forces pull the sweet spot toward decentralization. Apache, eMule, and Skype all deliver information more efficiently and cheaply than their centralized counterparts. Likewise, if people are doing something illegal or potentially embarrassing—in other words, if there's a reason for them to seek anonymity—the sweet spot is likely to move toward decentralization as well. It was to preserve anonymity that AA, the Animal Liberation Front, eMule, and al Qaeda became decentralized.

But at the same time, other forces nudge the sweet spot toward centralization. Music lovers have gravitated to iTunes because it offers security and accountability. When you download a song from eMule, you just never know—it could be fine, or it could contain a malicious virus. But when you download a song from iTunes, you can rest assured that it's both legal and virus-free. When you buy something off craigslist, you hope and trust that the seller is honest, but you don't know for sure. On eBay, however, you can depend on user ratings, and you know that members aren't completely anonymous. When it comes to money, people want even more accountability—they use PayPal, for example, because it's a secure method of transferring funds online.

The more important security and accountability become in a given industry, the more likely it is that the sweet spot will tend toward centralization. People are especially prone to seek security when a service is unfamiliar. For several years, for example, Yahoo was king of the search world. At the time, the Web was new to most people, and they wanted a secure and accountable source of information. Yahoo delivered just that. It launched a central portal where users could get their stock quotes, play games, or check the weather, and it hired editors to create search categories and catalog a massive number of Web pages. You could trust Yahoo. If you were looking for a Web site about Hawaii, you'd get a pretty good match, and you'd avoid sites with unsavory content—unless, of course, that's what you were looking for. Yahoo was there to hold your hand.

But as the Web grew and users became more sophisticated, Google's new, more decentralized approach was very appealing. The site's search algorithms, which depend on user input rather than on editorial experts, produced more relevant results. Google replaced Yahoo's expert editors with a decentralized solution. The sweet spot in the search industry is still fluid, and it's hard to tell whether it's heading in one direction or the other. It's possible that a new entrant will offer a more decentralized solution (say, an eMule-esque solution to search), or that someone will create a hybrid between Wikipedia and Google. Or Google may keep its place atop the sweet spot. It's hard to tell where the decentralized winds will blow, but it's always wise to chase that sometimes elusive sweet spot.

CHAPTER 9

The New World

Hard as it is to imagine today, the Soviet government in 1917 was relatively up with the times. It had come out ahead in a revolution that overthrew an unpopular czar, and it had made modernization a priority. Despite their move toward modernism, however, the Soviets made some strange decisions. Take, for example, their reaction to the new technology of the time. As Paul Starr explains in *The Creation of the Media*, "After taking power in 1917, the new Soviet rulers could have invested in telephone networks, as other nations were doing at that time, but chose instead to emphasize another emerging communication technology—loudspeakers."

Yes, loudspeakers. Instead of wiring the nation for telephones, the Soviets set up countless loudspeakers across the country. That way, if they wanted to deliver a message to the masses, be it a patriotic song or a Communist Party speech, they could do so quickly and efficiently. "Down to its collapse in 1991," Starr adds, "the Soviet Union and the countries under its control had markedly fewer telephones than the countries of Western Europe and North America." The Soviet government failed not only to recognize a new technology but also to see that the world was rapidly changing. The czarist mentality of the previous century still prevailed. The Soviets focused on technology that reflected imperial values: higher-ups telling the common people what to do. But in the twentieth century, communication between individuals was far more important for economic growth than communication between governmental authorities and the masses.

Before we judge the Soviets too quickly, it's important to realize that when the rules of the game suddenly change, as they did with the popularization of the telephone, it's easy to be left behind. We're used to having things operate in a certain way. We learn the rules and don't anticipate radical change. That's why the French, for example, after fighting World War I in muddy trenches along the Western Front, decided to be well prepared for World War II. They poured resources into the construction of the Maginot Line, a series of forts and expansive tunnels that spanned over one hundred kilometers. The Maginot Line might have worked well in World War I, but twenty-two years later it was no match for the German army and its new weapons. The expensive, old-fashioned trench system was useless. Technology had changed the rules of warfare, and within a matter of weeks the Germans had full control of France.

Just as the telephone changed communications and technology changed warfare, the forces of decentralization have created a new set of rules. This change has been so rapid that industries and governments have found themselves employing outdated strategies. In going after the P2P music-swappers, MGM was using tactics that might have worked against a centralized opponent, but against a decentralized foe just made the problem worse. The French investors asked David Garrison who was the president of the Internet because they were used to looking at organizations with rigid hierarchical structures. GM didn't change its assembly line because it had worked well for so many years—that is, until Toyota came along. As we looked at these cases, we began seeing new patterns. Some have been surprising, and many have at first seemed counterintuitive. One thing's for sure, though—there are new rules to the game.

RULE 1: Diseconomies of Scale

Traditionally, the bigger the company or institution, the more power it could wield. In the past, small players might have had the advantage of being flexible, but the safe bet would have been on the big guns.

Decentralization has changed everything. AT&T was huge, had massive infrastructure, and employed tens of thousands. Skype had just a few employees and a handful of PCs to its name. Because Skype didn't have to support a large payroll, a marketing budget, or expansive facilities, it could thrive on minimal revenues. This lean approach, combined with a large, decentralized network of users, enabled it to wreak havoc on the phone industry.

As counterintuitive as this sounds, it can be better to be small.

Because it didn't have a physical company to support, eMule didn't mind that its millions of users were getting songs for free. Because Craig Newmark operated out of a tiny office in San Francisco, craigslist could list millions of items at no charge. Small size combined with a large network of users gives these companies both flexibility and power.

We have entered a new world where being small can provide a fundamental economic advantage. As diseconomies of scale increase, the cost of entering a new market dramatically decreases. How hard is it to start an online classified ad site? Not very. Size matters. The small rule.

RULE 2: The Network Effect

The network effect is the increase in the overall value of the network with the addition of each new member. Each additional telephone or fax machine makes all the other phones or fax machines in the world more worthwhile.

Historically, creating the network effect could be tough. The fax network had to be built one expensive fax machine at a time. Starfish organizations, however, are particularly well positioned to take advantage of the network effect. For some of the most successful starfish organizations, like Skype and craigslist, it costs absolutely nothing to add a new customer. While it used to cost millions or billions to create a significant network effect, for many starfish organizations the cost has gone down to zero.

Often without spending a dime, starfish organizations create communities where each new member adds value to the larger network. With every new eMule user, there's more music to be shared. Every new site on the World Wide Web makes the whole network richer with information.

Companies like eBay have used the network effect not only to survive but to thrive: buyers and sellers have stayed loyal to the site because of the value of network.

RULE 3: The Power of Chaos

As you read this, parents worldwide are beseeching their kids to clean their rooms. "How can you get anything done in this mess?" they ask. Similarly, the conventional thinking is that to run an organization you'd better be organized and structured.

But in the decentralized world, messy kids can rejoice. It pays to be chaotic. In seemingly chaotic systems, users are free to do whatever they want. Want to download a song? Sure, why not. Want to create a piece of software? Go for it. Want to write an article for Wikipedia? Be our guest. Want to create a Web site featuring your cat? Go right ahead. Want to drive a twenty-foot giraffe car? That's great!

Starfish systems are wonderful incubators for creative, destructive, innovative, or crazy ideas. Anything goes. Good ideas will attract more people, and in a circle they'll execute the plan. Institute order and rigid structure, and while you may achieve standardization, you'll also squelch creativity. Where creativity is valuable, learning to accept chaos is a must.

RULE 4: Knowledge at the Edge

In starfish organizations, knowledge is spread throughout the organization. Remember Ed Sheeran and the Labor Day hurricane of 1935? Because he was on the scene, Sheeran had better knowledge than his bosses back at headquarters. The best knowledge is often at the fringe of the organization.

Toyota understood this lesson and encouraged its assembly-line workers to innovate and make suggestions, since they knew better than anyone else what was actually happening on the line. IBM and Sun incorporated this lesson as well—they opened up their software and let engineers all over the world help make it better. Jimmy Wales understood that in some far corner of the world there was someone with unique knowledge about greyhounds, someone else who was an expert on South American history, and yet another person with frighteningly deep knowledge about Twinkies. Wikipedia allows them to share that knowledge.

RULE 5: Everyone Wants to Contribute

Not only do people throughout a starfish have knowledge, but they also have a fundamental desire to share and to contribute.

People come to Burning Man because it's based on a gift economy. They work year-round on human-powered Ferris wheels, pirate-ship school buses, and other art projects and installations just so the broader community can enjoy them. Contributors spend hours editing Wikipedia articles because they want to make the site better, and accountants want to share their expertise on Intuit's TaxAlmanac.org. User "jpgm" contributes free reviews on Amazon, while software engineers stay up all night to improve the Apache code. It's all in the spirit of sharing and contributing.

RULE 6: Beware the Hydra Response

Yes, decentralized organizations are wonderful places for people to contribute, and yes, they elicit some touchy-feely sentiments. But take on a starfish and you'll be in for a surprise.

Attack a decentralized organization and you'll soon be reminded of Hydra, the many-headed beast of Greek mythology. If you cut off one head, two more will grow in its place. The Spanish learned this lesson the hard way when they fought the Apaches. When the record labels destroyed Napster, they got Kazaa and eMule. Go after al Qaeda's leadership, and the organization will only spread and proliferate. Cut off the arm of a starfish, and it will a grow a whole new body. As we've seen, there *are* ways to battle a decentralized organization. But for goodness' sake, don't try to cut off its head.

RULE 7: Catalysts Rule

It's no surprise that Cortés wanted to talk to Montezuma, the Aztec leader. We naturally want to know who's in charge, who can make things happen.

But when the Spanish encountered the Apaches, it was a different story. There was no Montezuma. Instead, the Nant'ans played the role of catalysts. They'd suggest a course of action, but then they'd let go. Although they don't conform to the CEO role, catalysts are crucial to decentralized organizations. But it's not because they run the show. Catalysts are important because, like Josh Sage, they inspire people to action. Like Auren Hoffman, they map out a network, and like David Martin (or Mary Poppins, for that matter), they know when it's time to let go. Catalysts have taken the world by storm. But watch out: if you turn a catalyst into a CEO, the entire network will be in jeopardy. Just ask the Apaches.

RULE 8: The Values *Are* the Organization

Ideology is the fuel that drives the decentralized organization. Groups like the Animal Liberation Front don't have paid staff, nor do they have much structure. At its core, the ALF is an ideology. Take away the ideology, and the starfish organization will crumble.

Most successful starfish organizations were started with what seemed at the time to be a radical ideology. Granville Sharp had the notion that slavery should be abolished; Pierre Omidyar had the idea that people are trustworthy; Bill W. believed that alcoholics could forgo the experts and instead help each other.

If you really want to change a decentralized organization, the best strategy is to alter the ideology of the members. It's how Jamii Bora fights terrorism in the slums of Africa, and how Future Generations builds communities in Afghanistan.

RULE 9: Measure, Monitor, and Manage

Just because starfish organizations tend to be ambiguous and chaotic doesn't mean that we can't measure their results. But when measuring a decentralized network, it's better, as the saying goes, to be vaguely right than precisely wrong. Even if we could, it wouldn't really matter if we were able to get a precise count of how many members are in a network. What matters more is looking at circles. How active are they? How distributed is the network? Are circles independent? What kind of connections do they have between them?

Likewise, when we monitor a starfish organization, we ask questions like: How's the circle's health? Do members continue participating? Is the network growing? Is it spreading? Is it mutating? Is it becoming more or less decentralized?

Most catalysts understand these questions intuitively. They care about the members, but they don't expect reports or want control. Managing a decentralized network requires someone who can be a cross between an architect, a cheerleader, and an awestruck observer. In a starfish organization, people will do what they will do. At their best, catalysts connect people and maintain the drumbeat of the ideology.

RULE 10: Flatten or Be Flattened

There are ways to fight a decentralized organization. We can change members' ideology or try to centralize the organization. But often the best hope for survival if we can't beat them is to join them.

Increasingly, in order to survive, companies and institutions must take the hybrid approach. General Motors gave power to the workers on its assembly line. Jack Welch gave units independence at GE. Sun realized it had to give up control of its proprietary software.

In the digital world, decentralization will continue to change the face of industry and society. Fighting these forces of change is at best futile and at worst counterproductive. But these same forces can be harnessed for immense power: just ask the music-swappers, the Skype callers, the eBay merchants, the Wikipedia contributors, the craigslist community members, the recovering addicts, or anyone who's ever used the Internet.

Yes, decentralized organizations appear at first glance to be messy and chaotic. But when we begin to appreciate their full potential, what initially looked like entropy turns out to be one of the most powerful forces the world has seen.

EPILOGUE

Speaking Starfish Before this book was published, I never dreamed that I'd be on the phone with someone like Neil Cole, executive director, board member, and—in Starfish speak—Nant'an of Church Multiplication Associates (CMA). He told me about the "house" church movement, whose core principle is the power of circles. Everyone is in charge of the movement's success, and everyone is an integral participant. Neil had realized he was a part of a starfish and wanted to share that with me.

It's been exciting to see *Starfish* provide a language for people like Neil to describe their organizations. One vivid example is Emergency Services integrators (ESi) in Augusta, Georgia. ESi develops emergency management software for clients like Delta Airlines, the EPA, and the state of Maryland.

From the outside, ESi seems like a normal business, but a deeper look reveals starfish DNA: company-wide meetings where everyone is expected to be frank; open collaboration; and, of course, a team leadership model. The starfish concept reinforced what ESi had already known: there is power in open systems. This book served as a dictionary of sorts. "We never had the words for it before," explains Paul Butler, one of the company's owners, "but we realize now that we're a hybrid."

Initially, the power of starfish wasn't so apparent. When he first invested in ESi, Paul was wearing French investor glasses: "One of the things that we, as venture capitalists, hesitated about was that the founders didn't want titles; all three wanted to be equals . . . they didn't want anyone in charge."

In the beginning, Paul remembers, "people kept calling wanting to talk to the president or CEO. We would just tell them we don't have one. As we became successful, people started saying, wow, this must have contributed to your success."

The same starfish philosophy permeates ESi's software. Web-EOC is a crisis information management system that enables a starfish community of users. When an emergency hits, you want open communication and workers at the scene providing knowledge from the edge of the network. If only WebEOC had been around during the Labor Day Hurricane of 1939. It's inspiring to find hidden starfishes out there, making a difference in their respective fields.

The Apache story, in particular, has resonated in unexpected places. When my brother Rom told me about it, I wasn't sure publishers would be receptive. We mentioned the Apache briefly in the book proposal, almost as a footnote. But every publisher we met with loved the story and insisted we weave it into the book. The more we thought about it, the more the Apache had to tell.

Even before the book was published—just after advance copies were released—the phone started ringing. It felt strange to pick up and talk to generals from Special Forces. They were fascinated with Apache warfare tactics. Special Forces, themselves decentralized, have been effective in battling terrorist groups. The stark differences between the Apache and Spanish approaches to battle proved a helpful historical model for understanding the challenges facing military tacticians today.

And that's exactly it. Once you're familiar with starfish concepts, it's hard not to see the patterns play out everywhere you look.

—Ori Brafman

The Spread of the Starfish Revolution At

the prestigious TED conference in Monterey, California, a man walks into the bookstore and takes a look around. He then asks the staff, "I'm looking for one good book. What do you recommend?" The bookseller tells the gentleman "*The Starfish and the Spider*—it's the hottest book at TED—outselling everything and it's what everyone here is talking about. Some people are saying it's the best book they've ever read." The man buys the book and one music CD and walks out. His name? Bill Clinton.

Since the day this book launched, we have been astounded by three global mega trends: 1) interest in social networks and all other forms of decentralized networks worldwide, 2) a continued proliferation of starfish organizations appearing across a broad range of businesses, governments, and organizations, and 3) managers, leaders, and catalysts resonating with the starfish principles laid out in this book.

Somehow the book seems to have struck a chord in many. At Google, Mozilla, SUN Microsystems, YouTube, and many other companies, the buzz is spreading about starfish networks and how to leverage the power to build new businesses and enterprises.

When I met Lars Hinrichs, CEO of Xing.com, the world's leading business executive online network, at Digital Lifestyle Day in Germany, he stated, "This is the best book I've read since starting our company and it has had the greatest impact! After reading the analysis of the 'Catalyst versus the CEO' it became clear to me that we needed to have catalysts leading all key aspects of our business, and we adjusted our teams and strategy accordingly. It has had a major impact on our success. The company went public in December 2006 and is now worth in excess of $250 million."

Environmental Defense, the leading environmental group that coauthored the Kyoto protocol, asked me how to start a network of Silicon Valley CEOs engaged in environmental causes. Leveraging the principles in the book, they developed a starfishlike bipartisan network of top level business executives, the Environmental Markets Network, to interact with key congressmen and senators regarding binding global warming targets and caps in the United States.

The stories go on and on but some of the highlights are the priest and the executive of a large high tech company who both asked the same general question: How can I be a better starfish in what seems to be a spiderlike organization? We pointed them to the model of Mother Teresa, who created Missionaries of Charity, a starfishlike organization that has spread out to 133 countries, while still working within the confines of an ancient, hierarchical organization.

This book seems to have brought to light and made explicit what many people felt was happening implicitly, but lacked the framework and language to discuss. The starfish revolution is growing and is likely to continue unfolding over the coming years. Welcome to the starfish revolution.

—Rod A. Beckstrom

SOURCES

Introduction

The grandmother cell concept is discussed in Charles G. Gross, "Genealogy of the 'Grandmother Cell,'" *The Neuroscientist* 8 (2002): 512–18. You can read more about the grandmother cell and consciousness theory in a guest editorial piece by David Ross, "Some Reflections on (or by?) Grandmother Cells," *Perception* 25, no. 8 (1996), available online at: http://www.perceptionweb.com/perc0896/editorial.html.

CHAPTER 1: MGM's Mistake and the Apache Mystery

Metro-Goldwyn-Mayer Studios, Inc., et al., v. Grokster, Ltd., et al. was argued before the U.S. Supreme Court on March 29, 2005. The unanimous decision in favor of MGM was delivered on June 27, 2005.

Tom Nevins discusses decentralized features of the Apaches in the introduction to Helge Ingstad, *The Apache Indians: In Search of the Missing Tribe* (Lincoln: University of Nebraska Press, 2004). We learned more about how the Apaches survived against the Spanish when we interviewed Nevins ourselves. He described how decentralized elements still define the Apaches. For instance, Nevins shared with us his observation that coming-of-age ceremonies for young women further decentralize Apache ties because new, flat connections between the young woman's family and other clans emerge. He also explained that the Apaches use a gift economy in which all members of a clan, including visitors such as Nevins, are expected to share resources.

One fascinating book about the clash of cultures between Southwest American Indians and white settlers is Scott Zesch, *The Captured: A True Story of Abduction by Indians on the Texas Frontier* (New York: St. Martin's Press, 2004). Zesch's own ancestor was kidnapped as a child by a Native American group.

The South American indigenous empires of the Aztec and the Inca were much more complex than most people realize. In some ways, they resembled the political structure of the Roman empire: wide taxation, slavery, and rebellious factions that were forcibly "adopted" into the empire. Some of those factions joined conquistadors such as Cortés to help overthrow their oppressors. Cortés's impression of Tenochtitlán is described in *Aztecs*, edited by Eduardo Matos Moctezuma and Felipe Solis Olguin (London: Royal Academy Books, 2003), pp. 16–17. There are many works that describe the societal and daily lives of the precolonial Aztecs and Incas. Two of these are *The Indian in Latin American History: Resistance, Resilience, and Acculturation*, edited by John E. Kicza (Wilmington, Del.: Scholarly Resources, 1993), and Warwick Bray, *Everyday Life of the Aztecs* (New York: Peter Bedrick Books, 1991).

Information about the music industry and its fight against piracy was drawn from Steve Knopper, "What Happens When the Record Biz Sues You," *Rolling Stone* (June 16, 2005), and Daniel Roth, "Catch Us if You Can," *Fortune* (February 9, 2004).

CHAPTER 2: The Spider, the Starfish, and the President of the Internet

To learn more about the starfish's decentralized nervous system, we recommend Jonathan Dale's concise, informative Web site: http://www. vsf.cape.com/~jdale/science/nervous.htm. You can learn more about the starfish's powers of regeneration and view a picture of the long-armed starfish at the Edge of Reef Web site: http://www.edge-of-reef. com/asteroidi/asteroidien.htm.

Willie Drye, *Storm of the Century: The Labor Day Hurricane of 1935* (Washington, D.C.: National Geographic Society, 2002), chronicles the events that unfolded when the 1935 Labor Day hurricane struck the Florida Keys. Drye describes the mindset on the ground, the governmental decisionmakers far away, and the bureaucratic mess that followed.

CHAPTER 3: A Sea of Starfish

Information about traffic on craigslist is derived from *Business Week*, August 15, 2005, and from craigslist's online facts and figures.

Merger talks between Village Voice Media and New Times Corporation were announced on October 24, 2005, by Village Voice in a press release entitled "Village Voice Media and New Times Media to Merge."

In his book *Rebel Code: Linux and the Open Source Revolution* (Boulder, Colo.: Perseus Books Group, 2001), Glyn Moody tells the story of the Apache software's evolution.

The study about Wikipedia's accuracy is described by Jim Jiles in "Internet Encyclopedias Go Head to Head," *Nature*, December 14, 2005.

CHAPTER 4: Standing on Five Legs

The stories of Granville Sharp and Thomas Clarkson are beautifully interwoven in Adam Hochschild's *Bury the Chains* (Boston:

Houghton Mifflin, 2005). The book follows the evolution of the abolitionist movement and provides a strong flavor of the struggles of the founders.

The friendship and professional collaboration between Elizabeth Cady Stanton and Susan B. Anthony are described in Ken Burns's documentary *Not for Ourselves Alone*, which is available on DVD and VHS. A book by the same title provides more thorough information. Quotes from Elizabeth Cady Stanton are taken from her memoir, *Eighty Years and More* (1898; reprint, Humanity Books, 2002). She used the memoir to talk about her life and integrate her political views on women's rights. Some of Stanton's best writing can be found in her speech "Solitude of Self" (also available in book format), in which she advocates for the importance of women knowing how to be self-sufficient and existentially independent. Stanton's wit and intellectual criticism can be found in *The Woman's Bible* (1895; reprint, New York: Dover Publications, 2003), a popular book in its time that pushed the envelope on challenging the accepted roles of women.

CHAPTER 5: The Hidden Power of the Catalyst

The history of the Young Presidents' Organization is chronicled in Pat McNees, *YPO: The First Fifty Years* (Wilmington, Ohio: Orange Frazer Press, 1999).

The psychologist Carl Rogers was one of the pioneers of the humanist movement in psychology, which advocated for respectful and dignified interactions between therapists and their clients. Instead of being the know-it-all expert, the humanist clinician strove to allow clients to take an active role in their lives and become their own experts. In *A Way of Being* (Boston: Houghton Mifflin, 1980), Rogers delineates his "person-centered" approach and discusses the importance of being genuine and connecting with others on a deep level.

Lao-tzu was a legendary ancient Chinese philosopher who wrote *Tao Te Ching*. He is credited with being a founder of Taoism.

CHAPTER 6: Taking On Decentralization

Ingrid Newkirk's book about ALF activists is *Free the Animals: The Amazing Story of the Animal Liberation Front* (New York: Lantern Books, 2000).

The scientist fighting the starfish outbreak in the Great Barrier reef is Russell Reichelt, CEO of the CRC Reef Research Centre. You can learn more about his work at: http://www.reef.crc.org/au/about/staffdocs/RussellReichelt.html.

We altered the name of "Joseph" in the story about the al Qaeda cell in the Kibera slum in order to protect his identity.

Muhammad Yunus is credited with being the father of microlending. His book is *Banker to the Poor: Micro-Lending and the Battle Against World Poverty* (New York: Public Affairs, 2003). *Pathways Out of Poverty: Innovations in Microfinance for the Poorest Families* (Bloomfield, Conn.: Kumarian Press, 2002), edited by Sam Daley-Harris, also provides an excellent resource. An outstanding overview of housing finance for the poor is *Housing Microfinance: A Guide to Practice*, edited by Franck Daphnis and Bruce Ferguson (Bloomfield, Conn.: Kumarian Press, 2004).

An internal manual about al Qaeda's organizational structure and strategy was recovered from a Manchester apartment during a police raid. The translated text can be found on the U.S. Department of Justice Web site: http://www.usdoj.gov/ag/manualpart1_1.pdf.

The so-called *Big Book* published by AA is *Alcoholics Anonymous: The Story of How Many Thousands of Men and Women Have Recovered from Alcoholism*, 4th ed. (New York: AA World Services, Inc., 2001).

One of the best strategies we've seen to combat terrorism by changing the environment is laid out in Thomas P. M. Barnett, *The Pentagon's New Map: War and Peace in the Twenty-first Century* (New York: Putnam, 2004). Tom also came up with the Mafia metaphor.

CHAPTER 7: The Combo Special: The Hybrid Organization

EClass229 still offers unbelievable bargains for designer clothing. Since our coup with the Zegna suits, we've recommended it to all our friends.

The value of positive feedback on eBay is explained in Paul Resnick, Richard Zeckhauser, John Swanson, and Kate Lockwood, "The Value of Reputation on eBay: A Controlled Experiment," *Experimental Economics* (forthcoming).

A comprehensive overview of Google's history can be found in John Battelle's *The Search—How Google and Its Rivals Rewrote the Rules of Business and Transformed Our Culture* (New York: Portfolio, 2005).

The story of IBM's decision to give away its software is told by David Kirkpatrick in "Giving to Get More: IBM Shares Its Secrets," *Fortune* (August 22, 2005).

David Cooperrider has written extensively about appreciative inquiry. His titles include *Appreciative Inquiry: Rethinking Human Organization Toward a Positive Theory of Change* (Champaign, Ill.: Stipes Publishing, 1999); *Appreciative Inquiry Handbook: The First in a Series of AI Workbooks for Leaders of Change* (Williston, Vt.: Berrett-Koehler, 2004); and *Organizational Dimensions of Global Change: No Limits to Cooperation*, edited by Daniel L. Cooperrider and Jane E. Dutton (Thousand Oaks, Calif.: Sage Publications, 1999).

CHAPTER 8: In Search of the Sweet Spot

Peter Drucker writes about his experiences at GM in his book *Concept of the Corporation* (New York: John Day Co., 1972), pp. xxiv, 61, where he explains the key decentralized features and power structure at GM. Drucker reflected about his own life in *Adventures of a Bystander* (New York: John Wiley & Sons, 1994), p. 11, and described the people who influenced him. Drucker analyzed the politics of management in *Management: Tasks, Responsibilities, Practices* (New York: Harper & Row, 1973), pp. 248, 572–74, and recalled his influence on the Japanese in *The Frontiers of Management: Where Tomorrow's Decisions Are Being Shaped Today* (New York: Dutton, 1986), pp. 220–21, 224.

The business aspects of NUMMI, the GM plant that was managed by Toyota, can be found in the 1998 business case "New United Motors Manufacturing, Inc. (NUMMI)," written by Charles O'Reilly for the board of trustees of Leland Stanford Junior University.

CHAPTER 9: The New World

Paul Starr's *The Creation of the Media* (New York: Basic Books, 2004) offers a fascinating look into the decentralized history of the United States. The book juxtaposes European and American government policies on the media, postal services, and transportation. The author takes an informed perspective on national decisionmaking through decentralized and centralized lenses.

ACKNOWLEDGMENTS

This book would not have been possible without Rom Brafman, who collaborated with us every step of the way.

In 2005, the brilliant author Thomas Barnett offered to introduce us to his literary agent, Jennifer Gates of Zachary Shuster Harmsworth. After just one conversation, it was clear to us that she was the one. We thank Tom for introducing us; we thank Jennifer for her professional excellence, guidance, and warmth.

You can't have a book about decentralization without a catalyst. At Portfolio, our catalyst was Megan Casey, who, in Mary Poppins fashion, rode off on her umbrella to new adventures. In her stead, we couldn't have asked for a better champion than Adrienne Schultz. Her enthusiasm and support were a constant inspiration. Under Adrian Zackheim's leadership, the book took on its life—we thank him for telling us not to sound like nerds. The entire Portfolio team—Will Weisser, Liz Hazelton, Bruce Giffords, Cindy Buck, Branda Maholtz, and Nikil Saval—have been·a joy to work with.

We are indebted to our families for their continual support. Hilary Roberts wielded her red pen on countless drafts. Patrice, Elliott, and Emma provided love and acceptance throughout this process. We thank our parents and in-laws for their invaluable support and suggestions.

Kathy Smith has helped us keep our heads screwed on our shoulders for years. Josyn Herce, Manuel Lima, and Tom Maliska have been essential members of the team. We're fortunate to have incredibly smart friends like Denise Egri, Josh Rosenblum, Michael Breyer, Sara Olsen, Liz O'Donnell, Roberta Baskin, Werner Disse, Michael Danaher, Dave Wallack, Cort Worthington, Kimberly Caccavo, Peter Biffar, and Eddie Smith, each of whom gave us invaluable feedback.

We salute the CEOs, catalysts, and thinkers who have taken the time to share their knowledge and insights. These include Craig Newmark, Jim Buckmaster, Chris Gorog, Sam Yagan, Auren Hoffman, Josh Sage Thome, Deborah Alvarez-Rodriguez, Stewart Alsop, Ingrid Munro, Robin Wolaner, Tom Nevins, David Bradford, Jiggs Davis, David Garrison, Niklas Zennstrom, David Dorman, Scott Cook, Jimmy Wales, Scott McNealy, Daniel Taylor, Tim Draper, and Brian Greenberg.

We are grateful for the support of Stanford professor William Barnett, Chris Wing, Jessie Labor, Joseph Monteville, David Blatte, David Martin, Nancye Miller, John Doerr, Vinod Khosla, Loay Nazer, John Pritzker, Adnan Asdar, Sukie Shah, Andy Rachleff,

Bharat Doshi, Bonnie Serratore, Graham Power, Mark Schlosberg, Rob Rodin, Noah Kagan, Peter Simms, Michael Brown, and the Stanford/YPO program participants.

We acknowledge that most catalysts working for positive change remain under the radar. Our hats are off to them. Finally, we thank everyone else who helped make this book possible.

INDEX